PENNSYLVANIA
MOUNTAIN
LANDMARKS

Pennsylvania Mountain Landmarks

VOLUME 3

Jeffrey R. Frazier

an imprint of Sunbury Press, Inc.
Mechanicsburg, PA USA

an imprint of Sunbury Press, Inc.
Mechanicsburg, PA USA

Copyright © 2023 by Jeffrey R. Frazier.
Cover Copyright © 2023 by Sunbury Press, Inc.

Sunbury Press supports copyright. Copyright fuels creativity, encourages diverse voices, promotes free speech, and creates a vibrant culture. Thank you for buying an authorized edition of this book and for complying with copyright laws. Except for the quotation of short passages for the purpose of criticism and review, no part of this publication may be reproduced, scanned, or distributed in any form without permission. You are supporting writers and allowing Sunbury Press to continue to publish books for every reader. For information contact Sunbury Press, Inc., Subsidiary Rights Dept., PO Box 548, Boiling Springs, PA 17007 USA or legal@sunburypress.com.

For information about special discounts for bulk purchases, please contact Sunbury Press Orders Dept. at (855) 338-8359 or orders@sunburypress.com.

To request one of our authors for speaking engagements or book signings, please contact Sunbury Press Publicity Dept. at publicity@sunburypress.com.

FIRST CATAMOUNT PRESS EDITION: October 2023

Set in Adobe Garamond | Interior design by Crystal Devine | Cover by Lawrence Knorr | Edited by Lawrence Knorr.

Publisher's Cataloging-in-Publication Data
Names: Frazier, Jeffrey R., author.
Title: Pennsylvania mountain landmarks volume 3 / Jeffrey R. Frazier.
Description: First trade paperback edition. | Mechanicsburg, PA : Catamount Press, 2023.
Summary: Pennsylvania hikers know how rugged our mountain trails can be, but also how alluring they are; often causing us to wonder just what's around the next bend in the path. Just like in volumes 1 and 2, this third volume in the Pennsylvania Mountain Landmarks series provides some clues, and as in the other volumes also affords an armchair journey to some of the most unusual and inaccessible landmarks that can be found in the mountains of Pennsylvania.
Identifiers: ISBN : 979-8-88819-155-2 (paperback) | ISBN : 979-8-88819-156-9 (ePub).
Subjects: NATURE / Ecosystems & Habitats / Mountains | HISTORY / United States / State & Local / Middle Atlantic (DC, DE, MD, NJ, NY, PA) | SPORTS & RECREATION / Hiking.

Product of the United States of America
0 1 1 2 3 5 8 13 21 34 55

Continue the Enlightenment!

CONTENTS

Acknowledgments — vii
Introduction — 1

1. High Point Rock (Somerset County) — 5
2. Rothrock's Rock (Franklin County) — 12
3. General Benner's Rock (Centre County) — 18
4. Hexenkopf Rock (Northampton County) — 25
5. Castles in the Air (Centre et al.) — 33
6. Panther Rocks (Clearfield County) — 44
7. Bigler's Rocks (Clearfield County) — 54
8. The Old Improvement (Centre County) — 69
9. Satan's Handiwork (Lycoming et al.) — 79
10. Mysteries in Stone (Clinton et al.) — 87
11. Pennsylvania's Grand Canyon (Tioga/Lycoming) — 98
12. Rattlesnake Rock (Lycoming County) — 107

Unbelievable Postscript — 121
Bibliography — 123
About the Author — 125

ACKNOWLEDGMENTS

Both of my children have no children of their own, so I have no grandchildren. Most parents long to have that, and I guess I miss that somewhat. However, I have step-grandchildren who accepted me as such, which is gratifying. However, I've always thought that my books are my legacy and claim to immortality rather than tenuous family ties, which can disappear at the whims of fate. On the other hand, my children have made me proud of their college grades and subsequent employment success despite the sorrows and trials they had to go through in their lives. I want to acknowledge them for the pride they have expressed in me for my writing success. They continue to make me proud, and I hope I can continue to reciprocate in the future.

PROGRESS
(A lament for our planet.)

While peepers are chorusing from the woods' lonely bowers,
Clouds dance with the full moon, portending some showers.

The mountains slumber and dream of days past.
Wolves, elks, and panthers were not meant to last.

Indians and hardy pioneers are only memories of yore.
Mountain streams murmur of times that are no more.

The things of old have all faded away;
Now ghosts of the past hold full sway.

Final stragglers of day flee shadows of night.
Silence and stillness await morning light.

The mountains brood upon the forgotten past
and wonder how changes came so fast.

Now the rocks and hills cry out, "alas,"
and somberly reflect on what has come to pass.

Seeing what man has done in his dangerous game,
Nature wonders, "Does nothing ever stay the same?"

INTRODUCTION

As in the first two volumes of this series, this volume, the last in the series, provides an armchair journey to some of the most unusual and inaccessible landmarks in the mountains of Pennsylvania. And, like the others, these iconic spots are accessible only to rugged and determined seekers who can scale our sunny Alpine slopes or slog through dark swales in green-lit forests.

This type of journey was not daunting to our Native American brothers, who were used to traveling such paths long before the first white settlers arrived upon the scene. And those native sons were as easily impressed with the rock formations highlighted in the *Pennsylvania Mountain Landmarks* series as we are today. The Seneca Indians even had a name for such places, calling them *Tario*, or "beautiful rocks" (see page 445 in Uriah Cummings delightful narrative titled *The Song of U-RI-ON-TAH*).

Anyone who loves the natural world can identify with the Senecas' sentiments, and therefore it's not surprising to find that the Indians also often had myths and legends that they assigned to their *tario* places, stories that they told and retold around their campfires, and which in some cases have even come down to us in this, a more hurried and materialistic age.
But the ever-practical sons of the forest also recognized that such spectacular spots could not only serve as landmarks to find their way along their rich green mountain paths but also, in some cases, as places of shelter to serve as a refuge when the weather turned ugly and wild winds forced them to seek cover. Several such spots are highlighted in this and previous

volumes, so there is always that colorful touch of the Native American that adds so much to our appreciation of these landmarks.

Likewise, the reader will also find that the white settlers also generated tales and human interest episodes that still cling to these landmarks today. Many of the stories are not historically verifiable, being the oral histories and "tall tales" they often are. Nonetheless, they are a part of the local color of that area and, as such, are part of its cultural makeup. Therefore, it will be up to readers to decide just how much they want to accept as fact and how much as "fancy."

This was the same caveat I directed to my readers in my Pennsylvania Fireside Tales series, and it also seems appropriate for this volume. Particularly when the reader is confronted with the tales of the rocks once feared by early settlers in Northampton County called the Witch's Head or by the area in Pennsylvania's Grand Canyon once feared by Indians as the place of the wailing child.

These stories and the satisfaction of finding and visiting the places they told of spurred me onward all these past years. It has also been gratifying to plan my trips so that the weather is just right for getting the best photos of these remarkable places. I felt that the reader should be able to see some of what I saw in the best possible light and from the best possible angles. That is the reason, therefore, that the reader will find so many photographs in this and previous volumes.

The cover picture on this volume is of a section of Bilger's Rocks in the county park of that name in Clearfield County. Easily accessible, the rock city at the park is one of the most interesting I've ever explored. Reminiscent of scenes from the Jurassic Park movies, the place is filled with natural wonders and colorful tales. See Chapter 7 in this volume for the story.

Who doesn't enjoy such places and their stories? At least, it's hard for me to think otherwise, being the lover of the mountains that I am. Like Maria in *The Sound of Music* movie, my mind always tends to go to the hills whenever I want to find peace; whenever I physically go to them, I am not disappointed.

The sounds of the peepers in the spring always add a mellow note to that time of year, and pathways decorated with Golden Rod, Mullein, Queen Anne's Lace, Chickory, Rhododendron, Mountain Laurel, Columbine,

Lupine, Virginia Creeper and many other beautiful wildflowers, provide year-round color which soothes the soul.

Sounds of nature's rhapsody, the songs of birds, always remind me of the adventures I've had traversing twists and turns of mountain pathways bathed in genial sunshine while fleecy white clouds floated in a deep blue sky overhead. It is paradise enough for me while on this earth, and maybe I just talked myself into continuing my adventures and exploring some of the most unusual landmarks in our Pennsylvania mountains. I've identified more of them, places that seem to call. But I've got other books to write, so maybe they will have to wait for another adventurer who will write about them someday. More power to them!

CHAPTER 1

HIGH POINT ROCK

When considering places where I might find interesting rock formations in our Pennsylvania mountains, I knew I needed to visit Mount Davis in Somerset County. I'd never been to that county but had, years ago, decided I must go there someday after reading a poem by James Whitcomb Riley titled 'Mongst The Hills O' Somerset."

The poem's stirring verses are known to have been inspired by Riley's visit to the scenic mountains of the county sometimes called "the roof garden of Pennsylvania," and his stanzas capture the enchantment felt by many people when they admire any of Pennsylvania's Alpine slopes and hike up one of its airy mountains or down a rushing glen.

One lament in particular in Riley's poem,[1] "'MONGST the Hills O' Somerset Wisht I was a-roamin' yet!"

is as stirring as the verses of Robert Burns, the Scottish bard who pined in one of his most famous poems:

"*My heart's in the Highlands*, my heart is not here, *My heart's in the Highlands* a-chasing the deer. A chasin' the wild deer and following the roe, my hearts in the highlands wherever I go."[2]

Somerset County is notable for the high peaks of the Laurel and Allegheny Mountains that traverse it and which, when ascended, provide spectacularly expansive panoramas of seemingly endless ranges cascading off into the distance like blue waves on an undulating ocean. But one of those prominences stands out above the others.

---
1. See www.roberburns.org/works/290.shtml.
2. Found on the web at www.poetrynook.com/poem/mongst-hills-o-somerset.

A view of one of the crevices in Baughman Rocks

Designated as the highest point in Pennsylvania, the 3,213-foot-high Mt. Davis sounds impressive but somewhat disappointing. It does not tower above the surrounding mountain land, which never drops below 3,000 feet, but impressive views can be had by climbing the observation tower at the mountaintop, and here also are large sandstone boulders heaved to the surface by fluctuating freezes and thaws of over 200 million years. This created a unique "rock city," which geologists term "sorted stones" due to the patterns seemingly formed by the upheavals.[3]

---

3. Historical marker at Mount Davis; on the web at https://www.atlasobscura.com/places/mount-davis.

It was one of those stones that I came here to see. The one that claims the palm of being the highest point in the state. After having already climbed many of Pennsylvania's mountain peaks, I wanted to lay my hand on it and thereby make the legitimate claim that I had touched "the roof of Pennsylvania."[4]

It was not an easy place to find, and even locals were sometimes unsure how best to get there. But eventually, I did get there and achieved my goal (see pictures). However, there are also many historical plaques at this same spot, and they provided me with some interesting tales and legends that cling to this mountain today.

One plaque explains that Mt. Davis takes its name from one John Nelson Davis, a prominent citizen in the area. He was not only an ordained minister but also spent time as a surveyor, school teacher, farmer, and even served as 1st. Sergeant of Company K, 171st. Pennsylvania Volunteers, and was one of the last surviving Civil War Veterans of this area. His real passion was as a naturalist, with a particular fascination with Mt. Davis, so when it came time to name the mountain, it seemed fitting to name it after him.[5]

Yet another plaque reveals that Negro Mountain was so-named because it was here that Nemesis, a black frontiersman, was killed during the French and Indian War of the 1750s when fighting Indians beside borderer Thomas Cresap of Maryland. Local legends say that the night before he died, he confided to Cresap that he had a vivid premonition, a dream that he would die the following day.[6]

On this same mountain, almost one hundred years later, another tragic event became known as the story of the "Wild Child."

It seems that sometime in late spring or early summer of 1830, a family named Shultz worked a small farm on the slopes of Negro Mountain. They had a herd of cattle that they put out to pasture in the nearby woods every day, and at the end of each day, they sent their ten-year-old daughter, Lydia, to gather them up and lead them back to the barn before nightfall.

---

4. Ironic sidelight: Mt. Davis is no longer the most prominent landmark/place name in Somerset County. In September of 2001, the village of Shanksville in Stonycreek Township became infamous as the crash site of United Airlines Flight 93, which was taken over by Al Queda terrorists who deliberately crashed the plane there. Then, in July of 2002, the small village of Quecreek in Lincoln Township captured the nation's attention when eighteen coal miners were trapped in a flooded mine tunnel for three days before being rescued. All eighteen men survived the ordeal.
5. Historical marker at Mount Davis.
6. Historical sign along Interstate 68; on the web at http://www.whilbr.org/itemdetail.aspx?idEntry=3024.

One evening, the little girl went out to fetch the cows, but when night came and she had not returned, the Shultzs and their friends began a frantic search, but to no avail.

Months passed, and the family lost hope, even though reports surfaced occasionally about someone sighting a wild animal that they swore had to be the missing child since it almost looked human. Eventually, the "animal" was sighted more frequently, but in each case, it ran away when anyone tried to get close to it.

Finally, the family gained the "animal's" trust, realizing that it was their daughter Lydia, who had become quite wild, seemingly as wild as the bobcats, foxes, wolves and porcupines whose assorted weird cries she could hear every night that she had spent on the mountain. In her fear and desperation, she resorted to living off the land, surviving on wild berries, roots, and whatever else nature could provide. In that time, she had become fully "wild," and history does not say how long it took the Shultzs to domesticate the little girl so she could resume a normal life once again.[7]

In mentioning the legends and stories connected with this unique spot, I would be remiss if I didn't recall the legend of Baughman Rocks, even though it is quite an unsettling story that would no doubt have been forgotten save for an account found in the archives of the Somerset County Historical Society. It seems that in 1849 there was another family whose farm lay on or near the top of Negro Mountain in Elk Lick Township, and the legend in question concerns that family.

The Baughman homestead sat on the west side of a road that connected the village of Summit Mills and a small cluster of cabins known as the Peck Settlement. The site was lonely, with the nearest neighbor over a mile away. But that isolation was probably fine with Henry Baughman, and certainly so with his neighbors, who avoided him because he was known to have a "passionate temper."

He was a German immigrant and a tailor by trade, but he also raised several cows on his small holding. Besides he and his wife, who were both in their late thirties at the time of this episode, he also had a sixteen-year-old daughter, Elizabeth, a son, Henry, about fourteen, and a twelve-year-old son, August, and several younger children.

---

7. Blackburn and Welfley, *History of Bedford and Somerset Counties Pa.* Chapter 3 (Elk Lick Township); Also taken from a historical marker at Mount Davis.

The author with his hand on the "roof of Pennsylvania"

The father's ill temper reached new levels of fury one Saturday night when his cows, allowed to run at large, failed to come home. It was early April, and it had snowed heavily that day so that a covering of several inches lay on the ground. It made for good tracking snow, so Henry and his sons set out to find the missing livestock early Sunday morning.

The father was so frantic to find his cattle that he pressed his sons to go faster. However, August grew increasingly tired as they went along, and the father, becoming angrier and angrier as August continued to slow the search, hit him over the head with a large cudgel he was carrying.

The blow was so violent that it knocked August out. He lay so still that Henry thought he was dead, particularly since blood flowed from the child's nose and mouth. But rather than mourn over his injured son, the sadistic father's first thought was to conceal the evidence. They were at the mountaintop, and large piles of boulders with their many crevices and tunnels offered perfect hiding places for the body. Finding a crevice deeper and less obvious than the others, Baughman dragged his son's body over to it and dropped it in, all in the presence of his oldest son, Henry.

When they returned home, the murderer feigned dismay that August was not there. He claimed that Henry and August had started to race one another, but Henry had fallen while August kept running home, and that was the last time he had seen him. An immediate search was made around the homestead without avail, and so the next morning, when none of the Baughman's neighbors had seen the boy either, a search party went out to look for him.

By this time the sun had melted the snow, and no tracks were left to follow. For the entire week, search parties, swelling to over five hundred people, looked in every crevice, every dark thicket, and every hollow log and tree with no success. The following week, smaller search parties continued to look, but no trace of the boy was ever found. Even his father could not find him when he later returned alone to remove his son's hidden body from the crevice and bury it.

The absence of the corpse proved unsettling to the father and a mystery to all who had searched for it. What happened to August was never determined, and it remains a mystery. Since his son's body was never found, it was difficult to bring the father to trial, but on the testimony of his son Henry,

A view of some of the rocks behind High Point Rock

he was convicted and served a prison term of over eleven years. He doggedly maintained his innocence for the remainder of his life, but most of the township residents believed just as firmly that the man was guilty as charged.

Solomon Trassler may have proved them right several years later. Trassler, son of Silas Trassler, had been sent to the Pine Swamp, which was several miles away from where little Henry Baughman's body had been concealed in the rocks, to look for pine knots, which were good fire starters and fuel for handheld torches.

Trassler's searches took him in wide arcs about and in the swampy area until he was taken aback by a stark white object sticking out of the inky black mud. Further inspection revealed a human skull, and more digging uncovered a jaw bone and a few others. Subsequent medical evaluation concluded that they were the bones of a twelve to fourteen-year-old boy, and it was felt that they were likely those of August Baughman since he was the only known person to have disappeared near there in recent memory.

Locals agreed that no one had searched here when looking for August and that he must not have been killed by his father's blow after all. Most probably, he had been only stunned and, after regaining consciousness, tried to find his way back home. In his dazed state, he became lost in the Pine Swamp and expired there, too weak and exhausted to find his way out.

It was a tragedy that preyed on August's father's mind until his dying day and a story that became linked to the spot where it had occurred. To this day, the rocks where little August was concealed are known as Baughman Rocks. It remains a lonely and little-visited place, but if August Baughman's soul still clings to this spot, it is hoped that it will finally have found peace.[8]

LOCATION: Mt Davis is in Forbes State Forest near Markleton, Elk Lick Township, Somerset County (DD GPS Coordinates: 39.78587, -79.17672). Take the Route 219 bypass, and just north of Meyersdale, take the Mt. Davis Road / SR2004 exit. Follow Mt. Davis road toward the west and signs to Mt. Davis.

---

8. "The Legend of Baughman's Rock," unknown author, from the Somerset County Historical Society files.

CHAPTER 2

ROTHROCK'S ROCK

One of the most iconic photos of Pennsylvania's mountain landmarks was taken in Michaux State Forest in 1900. Michaux State Forest consists of over 85,000 acres of some of the most beautiful sections of the South Mountains in Adams, Franklin, and Cumberland Counties, with South Mountain being the northern terminus of the scenic Blue Ridge Mountains of northern Virginia.

To this day, Michaux is revered by Pennsylvania foresters as the "cradle" of the State Forestry Department, along with its resultant conservation and preservation efforts. For it was here, in May of 1903, that far-sighted Governor Samuel W. Pennypacker set up the Pennsylvania State Forestry Academy in Mount Alto.

It was one of the first such schools in the United States and joined the august ranks of those at Yale University in New Haven, Connecticut and George W. Vanderbilt's Biltmore estate near Ashville, North Carolina. The name of the state forest itself was chosen in honor of Andre Michaux, a French botanist who discovered and named many plant species here in the 1800s.[1]

Along with its vast variety of flora and fauna, Michaux also can boast of the many fine views that can be had from its mountaintops and a delightful network of hiking trails as well. There are also large boulders on the mountainsides that provide rock climbing challenges to the more adventuresome. But one rock, in particular, drew me here one fine spring

---

1. Found on the web at dcnr.pa.gov/StateForests/FindAForest/Michaux/.

Joseph Trimble Rothrock and his dog Rab at his famous rock in 1900.

day in 2018: the rock featured in an iconic photo taken at the turn of the eighteenth century.

As can be seen from the iconic photo of Jacob Trimble Rothrock standing at the rock he was to make famous, the rock in question is not ordinary. Likewise, the man standing next to it was also unique in his own right. He and his faithful canine companion Rab came here in 1900 to observe the toll that recent lumbering operations had taken on the South Mountains. The hillsides were barren, stripped of their timber without regard to aesthetics or environmental impact, and the man looking over those hillsides was planning to do something about it.

Today, our forests are classified as "second growth" since they've existed for less than one hundred years, thanks to the almost total extermination of the state's original virgin forests in the late nineteenth and early twentieth centuries. The resultant denuded look of the once-magnificent mountains was so bleak and depressing that the state's more forward-thinking conservationists, partly due to a public outcry by naturalists and hunters, knew that a more responsible approach was needed in forest management.

Among those visionaries was Dr. Joseph Trimble Rothrock, now hailed as the "Father of Pennsylvania Forestry," but whose original efforts were overshadowed by more notable environmentalists like Pennsylvania

Goal achieved! The author standing where J. T. Rothrock once stood.

governor Gifford Pinchot and President "Teddy" Roosevelt. Nevertheless, Joseph T. Rothrock's accomplishments were eventually recognized for their importance.[2]

Born in 1839 in the small community of McVeytown, Mifflin County, Pennsylvania, he came from modest beginnings. But despite his humble start, he subsequently showed that innate intelligence, hard work, and a good upbringing can propel a person to great heights.

---

2. Eleanor Maass, *Forestry Pioneer—The Life of Joseph Trimble Rothrock*.

The iconic image on the monument in McVeytown

His initial education was at the Tuscarora Academy, a local preparatory school, and his scholastic record there was so outstanding that it gained him entrance to Harvard University, where he studied botany. At the outbreak of the American Civil War, he was mustered into the 131st Pennsylvanian Volunteer Infantry, Company D, later rising to the rank of captain.

He participated in some of the war's bloodiest battles, including Antietam and Fredericksburg, where he was wounded. After being discharged from the army, he earned an M.D. degree at the University of Pennsylvania and subsequently served as a professor of botany at that same higher institution of learning.

Later, as a member of the prestigious American Philosophical Society, he presented many lectures on forestry and the condition of Pennsylvania's forests. In those addresses, he showed photographs of his many buckboard trips into northern Pennsylvania's abandoned and devastated forests. The photos highlighted how lumber companies had ravaged the woodlands and showed the soil erosion, flooding, and devastation of forest fires that were the subsequent result.

As a result of his increasing fame as a conservationist, he was contacted by two prominent Philadelphia women who were upset with what was happening to Pennsylvania's verdant heritage. Together, those three conceived that a society was needed to promote scientific forestry, which they founded in 1886. They called their society the Pennsylvania Forestry Association (PFA), which today promotes the goals established by its founders.

Rothrock's strong opinion that only the state had the resources and a mandate to restore the forests eventually won the day and was the rallying cry of the forestry movement. In 1893, he was appointed commission botanist as part of a state forestry commission, and he helped survey and recommend woodlands throughout the state that were considered worthy of preservation.

As the forestry movement grew in importance, he was promoted to be fully in charge of that commission and made a permanent employee of the State Forestry Department, which later was placed under the auspices of the Department of Agriculture. Here, he was accolated as the "Father of Pennsylvania Forestry."[3]

At the crossroads in McVeytown, a monument dedicated to Rothrock stands today. And on that same monument is a depiction of the iconic photo shown at the beginning of this chapter. However, I wondered if the rock in that photo is still in the same place today and, if so, what it looks like.

This curiosity caused my son and I to trek through the mountains near Mont Alto State Park in Franklin County to search for it on that fine spring day in 2018. My son and I had difficulty locating it, but once there, I wanted to assume the same pose at the rock that Rothrock had assumed in 1900.

---

3. Rebecca Swanger, "The Root of the Forestry Movement in Pennsylvania: J. T. Rothrock."

As seen from the best photo my son could take, that same scene could not be achieved. A large tree had grown up near the front of the mound on which the rock sits, and so the necessary angle was not attainable. Then, too, it appeared that some of the rock had broken off since Rothrock's time, and the rock itself may have tilted forward a bit.

It is now sometimes referred to as "Pulpit Rock," but park rangers and locals later confirmed that this was indeed Rothrock's Rock. Thus, it was gratifying to realize that I had done what many would never do: stand in the footprints of the man who helped preserve the very forests and mountaintop rock sculptures that are the subject of this book.

LOCATION: Rothrock's Rock is located in Michaux State Forest near Mount Alto State Park between Fayetteville and Waynesboro in Franklin County (DD GPS Coordinates: 39.8388, -77.5358). Off Route 30, take Route 233 South. Follow Route 233 past a fenced seedling area on the left. Look for a forest road on the left where the road bends sharply to the right. Walk about a half mile down this road, which becomes a trail, to see Rothrock's Rock on a high prominence on the right.

CHAPTER 3

GENERAL BENNER'S ROCK

Anyone who has traveled on the Benner Pike between Bellefonte and State College in Centre County will recall passing by the grounds of the State Correctional Institute at Rockview. The prison grounds are extensive, and those who might want to explore them are discouraged by numerous trespassing signs that warn them to stay away. Nonetheless, the name of the "Big House" that sits on the hill and is home to some of the worst criminal offenders in the state will no doubt invoke the question in the minds of many as to exactly where the rock might be that inspired that name,[1] and can it be "viewed" by the public today.

The answer to the question as to whether the rock can be seen today is that, yes, it can, just as in the past, but knowing where to look for it requires some vigilance. The rock sits along the west side of Spring Creek, and Rock Road parallels the creek on its east side, as does the Spring Creek Canyon Trail further down.

The trek along the creek is enjoyed by many hikers and cyclists, who are sometimes rewarded by sightings of Bald Eagles and Great Blue Herons who have made the canyon their nesting grounds. The easily navigated path winds between the creek and the towering limestone cliffs that form the walls of the creek's canyon. The path also eventually leads to a gated entrance to a State Fish Hatchery, said to be the most productive in the state as far as keeping Pennsylvania's streams well stocked with both native Brook Trout and Brown Trout.[2]

---
1. John Blair Linn, *History of Centre and Clinton Counties Pa.*, 256.
2. From a pamphlet titled "Protect Spring Creek Watershed," published by the Spring Creek Watershed Commission of State College, Pa.

One of the canyon cliffs. (Spring Creek Canyon)

This hatchery's efforts have been so successful that the fishing in nearby Spring Creek has almost become legendary in the minds of fishermen, who consider it one of the most productive trout fisheries in the state. In honor of that reputation, the state's Fish and Game Commission has given it the appealing name of Fisherman's Paradise.[3]

No doubt that name is enough to draw many to this spot, and visitors are not disappointed when they see the natural beauty preserved here.

---

[3]. Noted on a historical sign in Spring Creek Canyon along Spring Creek.

All those who hike, bike, or drive through this environmental wonder are inevitably awed by the dense forests on the mountain ridges, impressed by the lofty cliffs, and calmed by the soothing sounds of Spring Creek as it cascades over the rocks in the stream. But most of these visitors never realize that at one point, there is a historical tableau standing along the stream bank that points out one particular rock, or rock face, that is unique.

The marker is easy to miss if you are not looking for it, but once seen, it's well worth a stop to take a minute to read its message, which is headed by the words: Journey's End: "Here we will build Rock Forge," followed by "I had to pack provisions from the eastern counties through the woods to supply ninety-three people"—Philip Benner, 1793.

Then follows an account of how and why Benner came here:

> In 1792, Philip Benner purchased 1,000 acres of land along Spring Creek for its rich iron ore deposits. In spring 1793, Benner and 92 intrepid tradesmen, laborers, and adventure seekers trekked here on foot with pack horses some 200 miles from Chester County, Pennsylvania. Benner served in the Revolutionary War and rose to the rank of General. Some of the men were Benner's Revolutionary War cohorts. They endured great hardships, fording streams swollen by spring flooding and even cutting their own path through unbroken forest toward the end of their journey.
>
> They arrived and camped near the rock face in front of you on the banks of Spring Creek until shelters were built. They then began the construction of Rock Iron Works, which would become the largest industrial complex in central Pennsylvania at the time.

It took brave and determined individuals to make that 200-mile journey, and those qualities would prove even more necessary once they had arrived at their destination. In those early days, the forest was teeming with wild game, a mainstay of their daily diet. But it was also alive with bears, mountain lions, or "panthers," and wolves in such numbers that no man ever felt safe traveling alone after dark unless carrying his rifle for protection.

From that improbable start, Benner became one of the most successful and influential ironmasters of his day. In the years following his arrival

The Rock (Along Spring Creek, Benner Township, Centre County)

at the "Rock," he built two iron forges, a rolling mill, a nail factory, a gristmill, a sawmill, a slitting mill, and two iron furnaces in the township, which eventually bore his name. In those furnaces, the iron ore along Spring Creek was converted into pig iron bars, which Benner shipped to buyers as far west as Pittsburgh, as far east as Philadelphia, and even to Baltimore and New Orleans.[4]

Benner's skillful management and meticulous quality control resulted in pig iron that was of such purity that it was once heralded by Eli Whitney, that famous inventor of the cotton gin, as "some of the best in the world" and by buyers in Philadelphia as "the highest quality iron they had yet seen."[5]

The high quality of Benner's iron reflected his demand for perfection in his manufacturing process and his careful selection of employees. It is recalled that Benner's astute evaluation of a man's work habits included noticing the condition of the man's clothes.

---

4. Linn, *op. cit.*, 257.
5. Marianna Lee and Vivian Doty Hench, article "Centre County," *Pennsylvania Heritage,* March 1975.

The Rock. (A winter view)

In one such case, he noticed that the seat of a man's pantaloons was so well worn that he immediately sent him away, reasoning that "A man who sat down so much as to wear out the seat of his breeches was too lazy a man to be tolerated at Rock."[6]

In another similar case, he noticed that the cloth on the right shoulder of the man's coat was well-worn also. He sent him packing, too, telling him that "you are too fond of hunting to be a good workman."[7]

Similarly, it's reported that he was just as guarded when interviewing candidates for a job as one of his waggoneers. The men considered were expected to be skillful enough to drive a team of horses pulling a wagonload of Benner's pig iron over rough mountain roads to Pittsburgh.

In these cases, one of the General's make-or-break interview questions was whether or not the man had ever upset his wagon. If the man answered that he was too good a driver to have ever done so, Benner would dismiss

---

6. Linn, *op. cit.*, 178.
7. Ibid.

General Benner's Mansio, from an old post card (courtesy Nancy Lee Stover).

him on the spot, saying, "Well then, I do not think you will do, for you would not know what to do when you did upset. No man can drive from Rock to Pittsburgh without upsetting. No, you won't do at all!"

In addition to all his mills, Benner built his family a stately limestone mansion of baronial proportions that looked down upon the cliff face he had designated as "the Rock." The mansion and its "rock view" slowly fell into decay after Benner's wife died in 1827, and he followed in 1832.[8] It was finally razed in the 1940's. Even the ore pits here, where iron ore was excavated for Benner's furnaces, have been obliterated by natural forces, as have the foundations of the houses built for his employees.

Benner and his wife are buried in the Rock Cemetery, so named for the small community of the same name, settled by the workers employed in the various Rock Ironworks mills and shops. Their gravesites and tombstones can be found there today, but their memory, and that of Benner's "Rock," also live on in the name that the State Penitentiary near here has

---

8. Linn, *op. cit.*, 179.

adopted as its own. (See the chapter titled "Ghosts of the Graveyard" in the author's *Pennsylvania Fireside Tales Volume 7* for a story about the ghost that some say haunts the Rock Cemetery).[9]

LOCATION: General Benner's Rock can be found along Spring Creek in Benner Township of Centre County, about two miles southwest of Bellefonte (DD GPS Coordinates: 40.943611, -77.7872244). Take exit number 74 (Hospital exit) off Route 99 (there is a green airport sign with an arrow pointing toward the airport). Follow this exit road toward Penn State University, passing the hospital exit. Then, at the football stadium, take a right onto Fox Hollow Road toward the airport (there is also a green airport sign here). Continue on Fox Hollow Road into Patton Township and past the Toftrees Resort area. Then, continue past University Park Airport to a T intersection. Turn right onto Rock Road at the intersection. Follow Rock Road, and at a sharp bend to the right and on the left, there is a parking lot for the Pennsylvania Fish and Boat Commission. Pull in here and see Benner's Rock across the creek. The historic plaque is just outside the parking lot fence.

---

9. Much of the information about Philip Benner and his Rock Iron Works in this chapter was found in a series of articles written by Myrtle Magargel and published by the *Centre Daily Times* of State College, Pa., in 1940.

CHAPTER 4

HEXENKOPF ROCK

Geologists claim that some of the oldest exposed rocks in the United States are located in the "Hexenkopf complex" in Northampton County. But locals refer to this spot by another name, better known for a far different reason.

The small knob in this northeastern Pennsylvania county is one of its highest points and most celebrated annals of legend and folklore. And in consequence of those same lurid accounts, this very spot was once shunned by locals who feared the evil powers they believed were concentrated here.

The Pennsylvania Dutchman's name for the rocks, *Der Hexenkopf,* when translated into English means "the witches head" or "witches knob," and, as might be expected, it was so named by them because they believed that this was a place where local witches gathered to perform their nightly revels and worship their evil master, the devil himself.

Tales of witchcraft and hexes were once very common throughout the entire state, and I've preserved many such accounts in the stories found in my Pennsylvania Fireside Tales series (volumes one through eight). However, these types of stories seem to have been more commonly found in the Pennsylvania Dutch corners of the state, those sections that were originally settled by and had higher concentrations of immigrants from what is now Germany in the eighteenth century.

It is now accepted by folklorists and historians alike that these same immigrants came to the New World with the old superstitions and misconceptions that they had grown up with in the Old World, including the ancient beliefs in witchcraft and sorcery.

"Witches' Revelry during Walpurgis' Night." (Drawing by an unknown artist, 1668.)

For centuries, these superstitions had a firm hold on the Germanic people and almost all of Europe and had also become firmly implanted in the land. In Germany, in particular, the Harz Mountains were regarded with superstitious awe, especially the Brockenburg, the highest peak in that same range, where it was believed that this was a place to be avoided at all times because it was here that witches held their wild revels, especially on *Walpurgisnacht*; the thirtieth of April or the evening before the first of May.[1]

The heights of Brocken Mountain are not the most inviting, as seen in the following photo. The dark mist-filled forest and bizarre rock formations

---

1. Ned Heindel, *Hexenkopf—History, Healing, & Hexerei*, 15.

seem to add credence to the once widely-circulated tales of witches' gatherings here, and this no doubt deterred any but the most stout-hearted from exploring the God-forsaken place.

The strength in the beliefs that the Brocken was a tainted and unhallowed locale was addressed by folklorist Jacob Grimm in his treatise on Teutonic mythology, where he confirms that it was a place to be avoided at all costs and noted that in choosing a place for their revels, witches preferred spots where executions were meted out and blood was spilled.[2] The parallels to the legends surrounding Hexenkopf Rock in Northampton County are striking.

Early historians and local folklorists in Northampton County have preserved and investigated the basis for the many supernatural stories that even today seem to cling to this mysterious spot. Such tales are abundant, and one of the most curious is how locals were once awed and cowed on the nights when the rays of a pale yellow moon fell fully on the rocks and caused them to glow with an unnatural luminosity. It was especially on these nights, the nights when the Hexenkopf was "on fire," as locals sometimes described it, that many people were convinced that witches found it to be the ideal spot to gather and cavort in fiendish delight during their devil worship or witches' Sabbath.[3]

Geologists have, of course, explained this tendency of the rocks to glow in the dark from time to time, attributing this phenomenon to the fact that the surfaces of the rocks are abundantly embedded with flecks of mica, the silicate mineral that, by its very nature will reflect light that is cast upon it. The rocks would have been more exposed to that light and more visible from Stout's Valley to the south after local landowners, in search of ways to earn an income, timbered their Hexenkopf Rock forest plots in the late 1700s.

However, the tendency to regard the rocks with superstitious awe was not solely rooted in their geological makeup. Before the white man's arrival here in the early 1700s, there was once a thriving Native American presence in this area, the sons of the forest utilizing this same spot for hunting and as a source of jasper for their arrowheads and spear points. It was perhaps

---

2. Jacob Grimm, *Teutonic Mythology* (Volume 3), 1051.
3. Heindel, *op. cit.*, 71.

also a spot where they buried their dead since early explorers here claimed they found funereal-type mounds on the mountain slope.

Then, in the late eighteenth century, there were many ghostly tales about this isolated spot; colorful stories passed from one local family to the next, including one that dated back to the Revolutionary War. This particularly chilling rendition recalled that there was a strong wind that occasionally roared down from the rocky clefts of *Der Hexenkopf*, and those who listened closely to this "contagion" wind, as they called it, swore that in it, they could hear wails of the dead and the rattle of hoof beats clattering over the rocks.

The hoof beats, it was believed by many, were caused by a troop of phantom headless horsemen—ghosts of Revolutionary War soldiers who had somehow been decapitated in battle and then, for whatever reason, decided to set up their spectral headquarters on Hexenkopf. Then, in their restless state of limbo, particularly on dark and moonless nights, they felt compelled to patrol the township roads, their ghostly promenade sending chills down the spines of late-night travelers who might encounter them.[4]

These other-worldly associations most certainly would have fueled the wariness of residents to linger here when passing by the rocks, day or night. But, if so, then that reluctance was also stoked by their beliefs in witchcraft and their acceptance of its power. Those ideas were planted in their minds in the Old World from the time they were old enough to understand, and so they brought with them to their New World firm beliefs about *hexerei* (witchcraft, demons, and the black arts in general) and *braucherei* (faith-cures, white magic).[5]

It is therefore not surprising that in the regions of Pennsylvania that were settled by those same settlers, there could often be found practitioners of white magic, or brauchers, whose business it was to counteract the evil spells of supposed purveyors of the black arts, popularly known as witches or hexes. And the brauchers' techniques were as ancient as the beliefs in witches and witchcraft, derived from cabalistic rites practiced by medieval healers from time immemorial. So it's unsurprising that several noteworthy brauchers plied their sacred trade in the villages that grew up around the much-feared Hexenkopf Rock.

---

4. Heindel, *op.cit.*, 75-76.
5. Ned Heindel, *Hexenkopf—History, Healing, & Hexerei*, 15.

The Witch's Profile at Hexenkopf Rock. (Photo courtesy of Ned Heindel whose book, *Hexenkopf: History, Healing & Hexerei*, was the source for much of the information included in this chapter.

Two Williams Township families in particular, the Saylors and Wilhelms, became well known for their ability to effect cures using *braucherei*, with techniques based on the belief that illnesses had satanic origins and were carried on "contagion" winds or induced by the devil's minions; witches and demons whose sole purpose was to torture mankind, or in the Pennsylvania Dutchman's dialect *far die lied gwele*.[6]

---

6. Heindel, *op. cit.,* 25.

Standing on the Hexenkopf. The author exploring the wild scenery at the place that was once often avoided by those who feared its reputation as a gathering place of witches.

At some point, the practice of *braucherei* became known as pow-wowing, and brauchers were referred to as pow-wowers. Historians are at a loss to explain why this name change occurred since it more aptly applies to similar arts in American Indian cultures, but to this day, pow-wowing is still a source of comfort and cures for believers in the Pennsylvania Dutch sections of the state.

The brauchers of the olden time were just as convinced their methods would work as those who received them, and accounts of those cures, from stopping bloody noses to removing warts to effecting other more miraculous remedies, were widely circulated. Their methods had to be done precisely, with charms, herbs, incantations, and recitation of scriptural passages being ineffective unless administered at the correct time of day or under the correct phase of the moon, particularly that of a full moon.

It was under a full moon when the pow-wower believed his powers to be at their greatest, and it was then that he could best "draw out" the evil

A lady among the rocks at the Hexenkopf. My late wife amidst more of the wild scenery at the Hexenkopf that even today adds an aura of mystery to this spot that is still fabled in local legend and lore.

from a sick person and "cast it" into trees, animals, rocks or even into dead people. Such "transference" was believed to be an effective cure but caused the receptors of the evil to be eternally corrupted. Several of its pow-wowers in Williams Township chose the transference receptor Hexenkopf Rock.

The fact that the rocks were where pow-wowers sent the evil drawn out of their patients was well known to locals, adding to their dread of the remote spot. And that same spot has remained a source of mystery and suspicion for many, even into the twenty-first century. Accounts of fiery and acrid balls of smoke that appear among the rocks during violent thunderstorms are still reported to this day, said to be a result of a curse of hellfire and brimstone sworn on one another by two landowners who could not resolve their dispute over boundary lines around 1880.

There have also been reports of strange mists, unexplained disappearances, headless men, headless dogs, and other strange occurrences over the years, but as we've become more enlightened, these accounts are not given as much credence as in the past. Now, nature has once again reclaimed the rocky slopes, and visitors can find various herbs and plants that tend to grow here. But among these are some, like witch-hazel, fleabane, and rattlesnake fern, which, to those familiar with them, may still seem to make this an uninviting spot to many familiar with its history.

> **LOCATION:** **Hexenkopf Rock** can be found in Williams Township of Northampton County, about six miles south of Easton and near Riegelsville (DD GPS Coordinates: 40.6178776, -75.2412878). From the Interstate Route 78 exit for Easton, head south on Morgan Hill Road. About five miles down the road is Hexenkopf Road, on the right. Look for Hexenkopf Rock on the left as you head south on Hexenkopf Road.

CHAPTER 5

CASTLES IN THE AIR

One of my favorite things to do has always been to study topographical maps of Pennsylvania. When looking over these detailed elevational layouts of the mountainous regions of our state, I'm always fascinated by the names that have been assigned to little-known and out-of-the-way hollows, peaks, streams, and natural features that are hidden away amidst the many miles to wander that are available to us and, in most cases, only a short distance from our backyards.

As a result of those discoveries, and because of their proximity, I have found, and have been drawn to, many unusual places on Pennsylvania's mountain peaks. So it happened one day when looking at a "topo" map of Clinton County, I noticed a place on Nippenose Mountain called Castle Rocks. It immediately tweaked my curiosity, and as images of stately medieval castles and King Arthur's Camelot rushed into my mind, I knew I just had to see the place and include a chapter about it in this volume.

Located amidst Tiadaghton State Forest, the rocks stand in one of Pennsylvania's lesser-known state parks, and once I got there, I found a steep path up to them just off the parking lot of Ravensburg State Park. Although just a small and isolated park, Ravensburg was once home to a large community whose members would have caused their neighbors, had there been any, to complain about the noise.

The "settlement" to which I refer was along the rocky cliffs at the park's southern edge. The steep walls at this point form part of a gorge that Rauchtown Creek carved out. The rushing stream still flows through here

Raven (on left) versus crow. Seen in a display case at Leonard Harrison State Park in Tioga County, the cutouts show how much larger a raven is compared to its smaller cousin the crow.

and continues to add a touch of tranquil beauty to this wild country that was preserved in its natural state as a state park in the 1930s by the Civilian Conservation Corps of that day.

Back then, the CCC boys would have heard and seen the inhabitants of those rocky cliffs, and perhaps those same workers may have suggested the name for the park. Many of them would have recognized the avian inhabitants living here. For it was here that ravens, the much larger cousins of the crow, had for many years made these rocky clefts their roosting spot.

Notorious for their raucous cries, the birds could be heard day and night as if trying to warn off interlopers. And so it was decided by park officials that the park name should be based upon its most infamous residents, which can still be seen here from time to time today as they sometimes perch in their cliffside home.

It was with all these thoughts in mind that I first climbed up the Castle Rocks Trail, and later the Thousand Steps Trail, to the top of Nippenose

One of the castle towers at Castle Rocks, Nippenose Mountain, Clinton County.

Mountain to see the rocky promontories that look to some like the last remaining crenelated ramparts of a ruined medieval castle.[1] The tall sandstone spires, although nothing more than erosional products of countless freeze-thaw cycles typical of Pennsylvania's cold winters, are impressive but certainly not manmade. Thus, I was quite excited when I heard about another place with castle-like rocks that supposedly are of human construction and ancient origin.

When I first heard about the so-called "Roman Tower" on Tussey Mountain of Centre and Huntingdon Counties, I decided to see it myself. It proved hard to find, but after several frustrating "wild goose" chases, a hiking companion and I finally found it one thirty-degree day in mid-October. The drive out on Bear Meadows Road and into the Thickhead Wild Area was a pleasurable adventure, as its untamed mountains have always

---

1. *A Pennsylvania Recreational Guide for Ravensburg, McCalls Dam, and Sand Bridge State Parks*, Pennsylvania DCNR booklet available at State Park offices.

A wider view of Castle Rocks. At the top of the boulder field. They are hard to get close to, and so it's hard to get a good photo of them. The hike up the Thousand Steps Trail to the Mid State Trail proved to be particularly challenging and also fruitless as far as getting closer to the rocks for a better photo. Thus they remain as the silent and secure guardians of the mountaintop where they have stood for centuries.

beckoned me with a desire to learn more about the legends and tales of the olden times that color this wilderness even to this day.

Soon, we had to turn onto Laurel Run Road to head up the mountain, finally parking in a small parking area at the Mid State Trail trailhead. From there, it was an arduous hike up the mountain, our quest becoming more of an ordeal as snow flurries and stiff winds made our trek over the rocky Mid-State Trail a frigid experience. But when the tower was finally in sight, we forgot about our discomforts as our curiosity to see it close up drove us onward. Once there, we began to take photos of the unusual pile and could almost envision Roman legions standing guard around it.

But there seems to be no evidence as to who built this massive tower or why they did so, but since it does resemble a Medieval Roman tower-like one that still can be seen in York, England today (see photo below), it's not hard to guess why someone felt inspired to classify the Tussey Mountain

The author on the "Roman" Tower.

tower as a "Roman" Tower. That the Romans built it is fanciful since they never made it to Tussey Mountain!

So, my best guess is that some romantically inclined locals familiar with towers built by the Roman legions in their European conquests decided to name this one after those similarly-fashioned stone fortifications. But that leaves the question as to why the one on Tussey Mountain is there in the first place. The answer seems destined to remain a mystery, but seeing its construction and location on the mountain, it would appear to me that it could serve as an excellent deer stand or place where hunters could hide and wait for deer to come by during deer hunting season.

Maybe it was built for that purpose, but since its origins are destined to remain a mystery, I had to concede defeat and move on to other mountaintop castles and towers whose origins can be more readily ascertained. In fact, upon seeing the Roman Tower on Tussey Mountain, I was reminded of one I had once seen on another local mountain and whose origin was easily explained. Although this tower was not called a Roman tower, it

Multangular Roman Tower in York England. York was founded as a Roman fortress city named Eboracum in 71 AD. This military post was used by several emperors to launch campaigns across Britannia (present day Great Britain). As its strategic value grew, so did its strength. At first it was constructed with wood. By 300 AD, it was a large stone citadel. This Multangular Tower is one of the few remaining remnants. The 19 foot tall, ten-sided defense contained a catapult. On the right is part of a 76 foot Roman wall". (Caption and photo Copyright © 2016 Richard F. Ebert EncircleWorldPhotos.photoshelter.com. All Rights Reserved.)

nonetheless resembles one, and so it seems appropriate to mention it, as well as a nearby pinnacle of stone that sits on top of Nittany Mountain just above the town of Centre Hall in Centre County.

Some folklorists have claimed that this popular hiking destination was named after a local Indian princess named Nittanee, but historians have disputed that claim. Nonetheless, the name and its supposed provenance add a touch of mystery and appeal to the mountain, but several mountain landmarks here do so in a more tangible way.

Hikers and hunters trekking along Nittany Mountain sometimes stumble upon several impressive stone towers along the ridge top. The stone columns seem so out of place and obviously of human construction that anyone who stumbles upon them and knows that the mountain's name is supposedly of Native American origin immediately must wonder

J. Earnest Wagner and his "fort" on Nittany Mountain.

A secret hiding place inside the "fort."

whether the Indians built the towers. However, that is most certainly not the case.

As a young boy growing up in the shadow of Nittany Mountain, my friends and I loved exploring it and the surrounding mountains in a Tom Sawyer way. So it was that we became familiar with some of their well-kept secrets and allurements. These included spots like Council Rocks, Veiled Lady Cave, the Swing, Laurel Springs, Pennington Cemetery, and Bennie's Fort.

All of them proved to be irresistible places to explore for young boys looking for adventure, and eventually, we also learned the history and legends that cling to these places that, to young men, had such enthralling names. However, it wasn't until almost fifty years later that I was to delve into these tales more seriously and explore some of the spots from a more mature perspective.

The place we called Council Rocks was also said to have been built by Native Americans who once frequented the area, and that landmark is addressed in another chapter in this book (see the chapter titled "The Old Improvement"). But "Bennie's Fort" is of more recent origins and is not at all associated with the Native Americans who some think may have been its architects.

I had often heard that "Bennie's Fort" was built by the Centre Hall Troop 20 Boy Scouts, whose scoutmaster conceived the idea of building it as a project that would hold the interest of his spirited scouts and help work off their boundless energy in the late 1930s. Over fifty years later, I was gratified to learn that the scoutmaster was still living and quite hale and hardy. So I was even more gratified when he offered to guide me up to his "fort" and tell me more about it.

The old scoutmaster's real name was Earnest J. Wagner, but from the time he was young, he had acquired the nickname of "Bennie," which his scouts used when referring to him. They also decided that the most appropriate name for the "fort" he had them build should be "Bennie's Fort," and so after that always referred to it by that name.

According to the former school principal and Scout Master, he and his scouts just started the project that he would later complete himself. Once his days as a scoutmaster were over and his former scouts had become men,

A view of the 15- to 20-foot high obelisk tower built by Mr. Wagner on Nittany Mountain.

Wagner decided to continue building his "fort" on his own, mainly to get some physical exercise after sitting behind a desk on workdays. It was not a project looked upon favorably by his wife, who, he noted, told him his time would be better spent building them a house!

But the hardy outdoorsman had always liked the ancient medieval stone towers he had seen pictures of. He had also enjoyed a story he had once read in Harpers Monthly Magazine about a boy and a stone tower he built.[2] Thusly inspired, the Centre Hall resident kept at his project until his "fort" was completed. Then he built a much taller stand-alone tapering

---

2. Forrest Crissey, "The Tower of Revolt," appeared on page 346 of Vol. CXXIV, Dec. 11, 1911, issue of *Harpers Monthly Mag.*

A view of yet a third tower. Also built by Mr. Wagner near his "fort" on Nittany Mountain, it is 10- to 15-feet high.

obelisk of layer upon layer of rocks delicately arranged not to be so unbalanced that it would become top-heavy and tumble over.

The sizes of many of the stones in the main tower, which was the tower that became known as the fort, are amazing, and it would seem that only heavy machines could have moved them into place. But sheer determination and a chestnut pry pole were all that was required. It was also a matter of luck that the builder never suffered more than a few scrapes, bruises, broken bones or twisted ankles. And, despite the rock-covered mountainside with its dark crannies and crevices, he never encountered any snakes—poisonous or otherwise.

It was a labor of love, and he still wanted to continue his project even on the day he guided me up to the towers. We approached the tall obelisk tower after viewing the "fort" tower. Once there, the old Scout Master found a bread loaf-sized rock and tossed it in the air with a heave. It landed perfectly on top of the obelisk and stayed there. It was a perfect way to end the tour and, as it turned out, his life, as he died peacefully 14 years later, knowing the memory of his fort would be preserved in my books.

LOCATIONS:

Ravensburg State Park is in Tiadaghton State Forest of Clinton County (DD GPS Coordinates: 41.1084, -77.2436). The park is located 8 miles southeast of Jersey Shore. Take exit 192 off of Interstate 80, and head south on Route 880. Look for the signs for the park entrance on the left.

The Roman Tower can be found just off the Mid State Trail in the Thickhead Wild Area on Tussey Mountain of Centre County (DD GPS Coordinates: 40.7300648, -77.7330525). Follow Route 322 East from State College. Look for the sign for Bear Meadows Road on the right (Elks Club Road and the Mountain View Country Club is on the left). Turn right onto Bear Meadows Road and follow it past the Galbraith Gap Parking lot, and after a sharp turn to the left, look for Laurel Run Road off to the right. Follow Laurel Run Road up the mountain until it makes another sharp turn to the left. Follow the road to the left until you reach a parking lot on the right. Here, you can get on the Mid-State Trail and head off to the east. After about five miles, a sign shows the path to the Roman Tower.

Bennie's "Fort" and towers stand near the top of Nittany Mountain, above the town of Centre Hall in Centre County (DD GPS Coordinates: 40.839829974, -77.68416393). From Centre Hall, follow Route 144 toward Pleasant Gap to the top of Nittany Mountain. Look for the Garbrick Amusements barns on the left as you ascend the mountain. The fort and towers are on the mountain slightly above and to the east, but there is no path to get there, nor any parking areas below them. They are on the first "bench" of the mountain, and when there, you can look down directly onto Church Street in the town below.

FOOTNOTE: After completing this chapter, I mentioned the Roman Tower on Tussey Mountain to a hiking friend, who informed me that he had once heard that the belief in the State College area was that students enlisted by Thomas Thwaites to help him clear the Mid State trail over Tussey Mountain built the tower in their spare time. Tom Thwaites, who I have aptly named the "grandfather of the Mid State Trail," much to his delight, would have needed help to create that trail, and the energetic students who provided that help would no doubt have had the extra energy to build a stone tower with the stones they cleared from the trail itself. A comparison with a "true" Roman tower in England should prove interesting to readers (see photo of the Multangular Roman Tower).

CHAPTER 6

PANTHER ROCKS

There is still a lot of controversy as to whether the mountain lion has returned to inhabit the mountains of Pennsylvania. But ongoing sightings by experienced hunters and indisputable trail-cam photos all point to the fact that it has, or at least, passes through from time to time. If so, then it has returned to its old haunts. Once the dominant predator at the top of the food chain in Pennsylvania, the mountain lion was eventually exterminated here by early settlers who, in the interest of protecting their families and livestock from its attacks, killed every one they could find.

Thus, by 1910, due to the unchecked slaughter, this formidable "king of the forest" was reduced to a memory here and regaled as a past trophy of the hunt by those who once referred to them by names other than mountain lion. The nicknames varied from "panther" to "painter," among others,[1] and so the many mountain hollows, streams, and valleys that were once their favorite haunts bear their names today. Consequently, we find Panther Hollow, Panther Valley, Painter Run, and other such names scattered throughout the state, including the picturesque Panther Rocks at S. B. Elliott State Park in Pine Township of Clearfield County.

Clearfield County was once home to the great beasts that hunters wanted to count among their trophies of the chase, and so the historical record of that county contains many accounts of early settlers' encounters with, and killing of, wolves and mountain lions. These narratives describe

---

1. M. Wrobel, *Dictionary of Mammals*, 179.

what seem to be almost super-human feats of survival, and there is probably no better example of this than the tale of Benjamin Bloom's panther.

Bloom's father was a Revolutionary soldier who came from New Jersey in the spring of 1801 and built a log cabin at the mouth of Anderson Creek near present-day Curwensville, becoming one of the first settlers in Clearfield County. Accompanying William Bloom were his daughter Elizabeth, aged 16, and his sons John, age 14, and Benjamin, who was about ten years old at that time.

After building his cabin and planting crops, the father left all three children to fend for themselves and returned to retrieve his wife and other children. Somehow, the three children survived through the winter, subsisting on boiled turnips, handouts from neighbors, and the benevolence of friendly Indians. Later in life, the children would recall how, driven by starvation one day, they walked through four feet of snow to ask a neighboring family for help. They were given a large chunk of cornbread, which they managed to make last for two weeks!

Though a bit off-topic, the preceding narrative seemed necessary to show how Ben Bloom, after growing up, was tough enough to engage a mountain lion in hand-to-claw combat one perilous day. According to the same family accounts, Ben had a large mastiff that always accompanied him on his hunts when he was middle-aged.

One day, he took his dog out on a hunt, and it wasn't long before the dog picked up the scent of an animal and began tracking it. The hunt continued for some time, eventually ending in a large assembly of boulders, later to become the site of a stone quarry above Curwensville. The rock city concealed many lairs and tight passageways, ideal hiding places for large animal dens.

The rocks were situated at the edge of a ledge, and when the hunter looked down, he could see a large panther crouched in a rocky crevice. Then the dog spotted it too and, never knowing any fear, jumped down on the big cat. A terrible fight ensued, but with the dog and panther entangled in such a tight death struggle, Ben could not shoot for fear of killing his gritty dog.

Knowing the canine to be tenacious, Ben realized it would never release its hold on the panther, so he jumped right down into the fray and grabbed the panther by its hind legs with his bare hands. Then, between the dog's

Panther Rocks, a winter view.

Panther Rocks, a nice spot for a panther's den.

Panther Rocks, and another den spot.

Panther Rocks, in the grip of the cold winds of winter.

grip on the panther's throat and Ben's pulling on its hind legs, they eventually wore it down and killed it. That would have been a harrowing experience for any man, and later in life, when he began to experience tremors, Ben claimed his shaking nerves were brought on by his terrible struggle with the panther on the rocks.[2]

Clearfield County in the early 1800s was also home to other relentless hunters, one who in his day earned the title of "the king hunter" of that county. William Long claimed to have killed 3,500 deer, 2,000 wolves and 50 panthers in his hunting career.[3] How many of those panther kills involved any struggles with the beasts like the struggle claimed by Ben Bloom is not recorded, but wolf hunter Michael Scheffer claimed he had at least one that was similar.

Scheffer's story, which he said occurred south of present-day Dubois along Sandy Creek in Brady Township, was told and retold by his descendants over the years, and so it could have been embellished or inadvertently revised over time.

Nonetheless, the version that has come down to us today relates that the story "Mike" Scheffer always told was that one Sunday in late summer or early autumn around 1823, he had gone out to check a trap he had set for wolves along the banks of Sandy Creek. After walking through a large beaver dam on the creek, he came to where he had set the trap but found it was gone.

Then he noticed the drag marks of the grappling hook that had been used to anchor the trap. The veteran hunter followed them to a large fallen tree, one end resting on another fallen tree so that it was not lying flat on the ground. The tracks he was following seemed to lead onto the fallen tree, so Scheffer got up on it to look for further traces of the trap.

Just as he did so, he noticed a large panther lying beneath the tree and looking fiercely up at him. The danger that confronted him spurred Scheffer into action, especially since he was unarmed, and with a sudden burst of adrenaline, he jumped off the log, grabbed a small uprooted hemlock tree, and broke off the top and branches, thus fashioning a sturdy cudgel.

---

2. T.L. Wall, *Clearfield County Pa. Present and Past*, 20-41.
3. W.J. McKnight, *Pioneer Outline History of Northwestern Pennsylvania*, 166.

He then jumped back on the log and used his "war club," as he was later to describe it, to knock out the brains of the panther. The brave pioneer then used his hunting knife to cut off the panther's head, washing off the bloody knife in the creek. At that point, he noticed his schoolteacher neighbor, Whitson Cooper, approaching him through the woods with his head down as if thinking of other things.

Knowing Cooper had not seen him, Scheffer concealed himself along the creekside path while holding the panther's head. Then, just as Cooper was about to pass by him, Scheffer tossed the panther's head out in front of him. Scheffer would laughingly recall that Cooper's shock was so great that he turned ghostly pale and could not speak for several minutes. It was an understandable reaction when it was considered that, when measured, the length of the panther was determined to be eight feet and several inches.[4]

Wolves were just as formidable to early settlers in Clearfield County in those days as the mountain lions. Mrs. Charles Grassley of Clinton County, wife of hunter Charles Grassley, confirmed as much in the following letter, dated May 1928:

> I was born on January 2, 1845, at Penfield, Clearfield County, then in the heart of an almost untouched virgin forest. My father, William Hicks, of Scotch-Irish descent, was born on Hicks Run and was a professional hunter.
>
> He considered it almost beneath his dignity to kill deer, confining himself to elks. He was also a wolf hunter and was successful in his efforts to outwit the 'long tails,' as they were called. We used to hear them howling on the sides of the mountains near our home every night, and when we went to school through the deep forest, they sometimes followed us, and we often saw their tracks in the snow. Once, a pack of wolves, in the spring of the year, came into our barnyard and killed seven nice lambs.
>
> There were wolves about Penfield until I left there about 1865, and they did not seem to diminish in numbers until the woodsmen made inroads in the forests. But it was such a vast forest region that

---

4. L. C. Aldrich, *History of Clearfield County, Pa.*, 459.

The Panther Cliffs. Found along Treaster Valley Road in Treaster Valley of Mifflin County, early settlers recalled that at this place there were once dens of tawny mountain lions that sheltered here to survive the bitter winds of winter.

they could hide in there longer than in most of the wilder sections of Pennsylvania.[5]

These stories substantiate that wolves and mountain lions once roamed the wilds of Clearfield County, with the mountain lions presumably finding ideal nesting sites in the many rock fissures on Clearfield County mountain tops. Therefore, it would seem likely that these formidable beasts would have found the many crevices, cavern-like hollows, and deep fissures in Panther Rocks at S. B. Elliott State Park an ideal place to make their dens and to shelter themselves from the soaking rains of spring and the harsh winds of winter. Their prevalence here undoubtedly led early settlers to name those rocks after them.

---

5. Dorothy E. Shultz, synopsis of Henry W. Shoemaker letters and unpublished stories found in a box donated to the Society, *Journal of the Lycoming County Historical Society*, Volume XVI, Number 1, Spring 1980, page 19.

Michael Scheffer (1790–1879) and son John (A rare photo of one of the first settlers in Clearfield County and one of its most-heralded panther hunters. (Photo courtesy of his descendants. Although of poor quality it is of such historical significance that we decided to include it in this chapter.)

An anecdote from the historical record of Leidy Township in Clinton County will give the reader a clearer understanding of how chilling the howls of wolves and screams of mountain lions could be inside an isolated mountain cabin in those days. According to that account: "In 1826 or 1827, or about that time, a Mr. Kelley, formerly of Ireland, came and constructed a rude dwelling house on the western side of Drury Swamp in the gloomy solitude of the mountain forests. He was the first settler between the river and Kettle Creek and experienced all the hardships and deprivations attending a pioneer life. Often would the still hours of the night be broken by the fierce howling of wolves and the panther's loud and terrific yells; protected by the darkness of night, they occasionally came prowling around the house, passing over the doorsteps, and making night hideous with their loud piercing screams."[6]

Another anecdote, as recalled by the same Michael Scheffer mentioned previously in this chapter, confirms that mountain lions once roamed the forests of current-day Clearfield County. It also shows what a novelty they were to settlers unfamiliar with them.

According to Scheffer (June 4, 1790—January 5, 1879), in an interview when he was in his 86th year, his family was, during the summer of 1812, one of the first to settle in the vicinity of present-day Dubois. They built a bark "shanty" along Sandy Lick Creek, and this is the "shanty" he refers to in his recollections, which affords us a graphic window into the life and times of the pioneers of the early nineteenth century.

In Scheffer's words, "We cleared about two acres on 'the ridge,' as we called it. One evening, when our dogs barked ferociously on 'the ridge,' my brother looked out from our 'shanty' and saw a strange-looking animal standing on a log. It was just about twilight. Father, Georg, Fred, and I went up. The dogs had now treed the animal. Fred shot at it, and it went up higher.

"We concluded to watch it all night. We remained a long while, but the night seemed long, so we felled a hemlock against the hemlock on which the animal was. It now came down; the 'tug of war' was commencing.

"One of the dogs caught it by the neck. Fred caught it by the tail. I had a hatchet with which I belabored the head, and father had an ax with which he struck effective blows in its ribs. At last, we killed it, not knowing what it was.

"The next day, I took a paw of the dead animal and went to Jacob Ogden to ask him what kind of animal it was. He got much excited when he saw the paw and exclaimed, 'You dumm Dutch! It is a panther! It might have killed you all!'

"I took the scalp and went to Squire McClure, on the Susquehanna River above Curwensville, to whom I made an affidavit that we killed the panther. He gave me a certificate, which I was to present to the county commissioners in Bellefonte—Clearfield County belonged to Centre

---

6. D. S. Maynard, *Historical View of Clinton County*, 174.

County then. The bounty was eight dollars, but I sold it to a man going to Bellefonte for seven dollars.[7]

> **LOCATION: Panther Rocks** are in Samuel B. Elliott State Park, which sits in the middle of Moshannon State Forest near Penfield, Clearfield County (DD GPS Coordinates: 41.11276, -78.52594). Turn onto Exit 111 on Interstate Route 80 and follow Route 153 north. Then turn right onto 4 Mile Road and take an immediate right onto Old Route 153. Follow signs to park and then to Panther Rocks.

---

7. Aldrich, *op. cit.*, 379.

CHAPTER 7

BILGER'S ROCKS

Along Interstate 80 in the Allegheny Mountains of Clearfield County, there is a point where the mountain heights rise to an elevation that becomes the highest point on that roadway east of the Mississippi River. Spectacular views and thickly forested mountain slopes offer pleasant scenery for those traveling through here, but although uplifting, those scenes aren't all that unique since many similar panoramas and thickly wooded forests are commonplace in the Commonwealth.

As a result, most travelers likely don't give the area much thought or even slow down to enjoy it. However, side roads off Route 80 here lead to some unique places well worth the diversion for lovers of nature and seekers of the odd and mysterious.

One such place was mentioned in our chapter titled "Panther Rocks," and south of there, in Bloom Township of that same county, is a spectacular Rock City that is even more impressive than the Panther Rocks in S. B. Elliott State Park. This area, called Bilger's Rocks, is located in a county park of the same name, near Lumber City, Grampian, Curwensville, and Clearfield, the county seat. Named after Jacob Bilger, a German settler who was the first owner of the rocks, the boulders here are thought to be at least 300 million years old, and when walking among them, it's easy to imagine that you've entered that prehistoric period.[1]

---

1. Cindy Ross, "Eclectic Exploration: Unusual Rocks," *Pennsylvania Magazine* March/April 2021, Vol. 44 No. 2, page 40.

The Indians' Fire Pit. It is believed that it was here that the Indians built their campfires and sheltered under the rocks in stormy weather. Park visitors, though discouraged from doing so, still build campfires in the fire ring lying under the massive boulder that serves as the "roof" of this ancient place.

Archeologists have studied this place and have not found dinosaur bones, but they have concluded that Paleo-Native Americans once sheltered here, huddling under natural rock shelters and in massive rooms created by the gigantic boulders that densely cluster here. The Indians' enclosed rock shelters must have afforded them some much-appreciated comfort in winter when they sat by their blazing campfires underneath the rock ceilings. Taking some of the soot formed on those rock ceilings by the Indians' campfires, archeologists carbon-dated it, and from that analysis, they concluded that the Indians were here at least 8,000 years ago.

Those same rooms and boulders are found here today, where acres of massive stones form confusing and confining passageways that seem to lead to nowhere and where dark cavernous openings appear at every turn. Their yawning maws are daunting and uninviting, as though they are almost daring an interloper to enter their mysterious depths. But subtle fears like

Clinging to life on the rocks. Trying to find life-sustaining water and nutrients in the soil that is hidden in the clefts below, tree roots snake along the rocks, resembling the tentacles of some prehistoric beast of ages past.

this do not keep curious hikers from entering the convoluted hallways of Bilger's Rocks and exploring its many "rooms" that have become fabled for their grandeur and legendary associations.

On my first visit here, the ground was covered in snow, and it did not appear safe to try to climb down to the base of the rocks where the best views can be found. Later, however, once the snow was gone, we found an easier and much safer ground-level trail that led us right into the midst of the rocks. Once we arrived, it seemed like we had entered a world where time had stood still, similar to the temple of Angkor Wat in the Cambodian jungle or a lost island where even dinosaurs might still be hiding in some of those dark recesses in the rocks.

Tangled vines on the multi-colored rock walls, large trees growing in their "rooms," and a patchwork of sunlight and shadow all combined to make this an awe-inspiring place that was both formidable and alluring. But those who had come before us must have felt the same way since they

The engraving on the rocks at Bilger's Rocks. Not as clear as it was when it was first created, due to weathering and moss overgrowth, this large artwork is still impressive yet today.

chose names for some of the "rooms" that were also both intimidating and appealing at the same time.

Some of those previous visitors had left evidence of their visits behind by chiseling their initials on the rock faces. Although graffiti like this is to be deplored, one such display stands out. Dated 1921, it features an outline of North and South America inside a large globe, and the words "THE WORLD IS LOOKING TO US" underneath, with the artist's initials, JWL, underneath that. Closer inspection reveals that there is also a human eye engraved here, and, in the lower left quadrant of the globe, the form of a woman sitting on a stone and mourning over what appears to be a dead body.

JWL, or John W. Larson, at the end of what was known at the time as The Great War, which we know today as World War One, apparently knew that North and South America were among the few places that the war had not torn up, and so felt that they were in the best position to help

The author in the Devil's Dining Room.

The pointing finger on the rocks. The pointing finger indicates the path to follow.

The Bear Cave and its warning skull and crossbones. Bears may have once made their dens here, and still are a nuisance in the park if trash it not properly disposed of.

the rest of the world recover from that horrendous global tragedy. From that belief, he must have been inspired to convey a message of hope in his carving while including accompanying images that indicated the pathos of that time.

But there are also less hopeful artifacts here in the form of the names given to some of the "rooms" formed by the boulders. For instance, the largest room is known as "The Devil's Dining Room," and a narrow passageway from there leads past "The Devil's Dungeon" and then on to "The Devil's Kitchen." Certainly, these are not the most inspirational titles, but they are typical of places like this, where early farmers, exasperated by finding rocky, barren ground instead of potential cropland, decided that the devil must have put it there as another way to torment mankind, and so assigned his name to parts of them.[2]

---

2. Kevin Patrick, *Pennsylvania Caves*, 196-197 and Shok, Holly, "The City of Rock," *Pennsylvania Center for the Book*, Summer 2009, (https://pabook.libraries.psu.edu/).

The warning skull and crossbones at the Bear Cave.

More roots throttling the rocks in a tight chokehold.

The Great Hall. The large room celebrated for its resemblance to a great hall in a Medieval English manor house, and where yellow beeches and mighty oak trees seemingly dance their eternal Minuet.

The woman and the lone wolf. The image of the wolf is faintly discernable in the lower left quadrant.

A Tight Squeeze. The author squeezing through that narrow crevice between the Devil's Dining Room and the Devil's Kitchen.

And as if to confirm that idea, another narrow passageway extends underground for about 25 feet. The pitch-black tunnel, while not a cave, is called the "Ice Cave" because ice can be found on its walls even up until the very hottest days of the summer.[3] The dark subterranean shaft and its ice-cold narrow confines serve as reminders of what some novelists have thought a descent into hell must be like. Thus, the very presence of that

---
3. Ibid.

The Little Lion. This king of the beasts, with its lordly mane, crouches along the Bilger's Rocks Trail, greeting those who are brave enough to explore the labyrinthine passageways. This is a natural "statue"; it was not sculpted by the hand of man!

tunnel could convince some that the rocks are not a very appealing place to be and so deter them from coming here even today.

But at the close of the eighteenth century and well into the nineteenth, there were other reasons that most assuredly kept all but the most stouthearted from venturing into this area, at least when traveling alone.

In those days, the forests here teemed with wild animals of all types, but one of the most formidable was the mountain lion, whose weird cries pierced the deepest hollows and loftiest rock crevices on every mountaintop. Then there were the packs of wolves whose heart-stopping howls seemed to make the earth tremble, and to those who have ever heard a pack in full cry, it is understandable why that would be so!

And it was in mid-winter when those howls would be the most frightening, particularly at the time of a full moon. The Native Americans knew that when the full moon arose in the middle of winter, the wolf packs found it the most difficult time of year to find sustenance. The hungry packs, driven by hunger, would become more emboldened and venture closer to Indian villages in search of food. The nightly howls of the seemingly bolder packs and their green eyes glowing in the light of the full mid-winter moon was an association that did not escape the notice of the sons of the forest, and thus, they came to call that same moon the "wolf moon."[4]

Early settlers here also learned that wolves were not only a threat and a nuisance in mid-winter but at any time of year. They, therefore, made it a practice to bring their herds of cattle and flocks of sheep in from their fields every night and shelter them in their barns to keep them from being eaten by wolf packs. It was a common exercise, and from it, there comes down to us the story of Mary Corrigan, a young mountain heroine whose nightly task was to fetch the family's team of oxen.

Thomas McClure came here from Cumberland County in a canoe, poling his entire way upriver until reaching the 500-acre plot he had purchased along the river near present-day Lumber City in 1799. Accompanying him was his indentured 11-year-old servant girl named Mary Corrigan. Some years later, as a teenager, she was tasked with going out to the field where the family's team of oxen was pastured and driving them back into the large log barn that stood on the land cleared for it.

One particular evening, the faithful girl went out to bring back the oxen but could not find them. Realizing that the animals had strayed quite far, she searched far and wide, and by the time she finally found them, it had grown quite late. Fearing she would be caught in the impenetrable darkness of the forest once the sun went down, her efforts to drive the animals back increased in intensity. But then the animals turned in a direction she thought was directly opposite to the way back home.

Despite her best efforts, she could not turn them around, and in their confusion, they broke away and ran off into the forbidding forest. With their uncanny sense of direction, the animals finally returned to the McClure barn, but Mary did not. As the day wore on, the family's concern grew, and eventually, they conveyed their fears to their neighbors.

Soon, a search party was scouring the woods for Mary. They hunted all day and found no trace of her, and a search that night also proved fruitless. The concerns then grew that a mountain lion or a wolf had killed her,

---

4. "Full Moon Names," published in *The Old Farmers Almanac* website, dated September 23, 2020.

Man's Best Friend. Sam and Alice McFarland could not have children of their own, and their dog Jiggs was the next best thing. When their beloved canine died in 1931 they created this carving to serve as its epitaph.

but Mr. McClure was not about to give up hope and conceived the idea of offering a reward for her discovery. He consequently stated that any stalwart and worthwhile man who found her might reap the reward and have her hand in marriage.

Several young men took up the challenge, but Dan McCracken was more determined than the others. The next morning, he packed enough food to last him for a three-day search and headed out into the forest. After an unsuccessful hunt through the woods, he headed up along the river, and when near Goose Island, he noticed small footprints in the mud along the shore.

His suspicions aroused, McCracken waded over to the island, and there he found Mary crouched next to a large fallen log which had provided shelter for her during the night she had spent there alone. When asked why she had decided to go over to the island in the first place, she confessed that on her first night in the woods, she had lain down to sleep but had been awakened by the sound of a large animal nosing around near her.

A Crazy Fissure. A huge crack in the rocks at Bilger's Rocks, rent by the unrelenting freeze/thaw cycles of nature.

She was relieved when it went away on its own, but the next night, when she came to the island in the river, she decided to wade over to it, recalling that she had often heard that wild animals avoided getting their feet wet like the devil avoided Holy Water. Thus, she decided the island would be a safe spot to stay.

The noble McCracken gave the starving girl his lunch and escorted her back home. Thomas McClure, relieved to see his charge safely returned, was true to his word, and so sometime later, Mary and McCracken, her knight in shining armor, were married in a simple mountain church in the same woods where Mary had lost her way. But by then, she most assuredly knew that she could find her way through life without ever being lost again now that she had her rescuer to share it with her.[5]

Whenever possible, I like to include some supporting evidence for the tales related in these chapters. In this case, the story of Mary Corrigan's nighttime ordeal on Goose Island is somewhat corroborated by an incident, said to have occurred in the 1770s, that is recorded in the history of Grugan Township of Clinton County as follows: "It is related of one of James Burney's daughters that when about fourteen years old, one evening she was sent after the cows; when after having gone about two miles up the river, a heavy rain set in, night came on, and being unable to proceed further, she took refuge under a projecting rock, where, surrounded by wolves, panthers, and wild-cats she passed the night."[6]

Bilger's rocks have also, you might say, had a "rocky" history of their own. Throughout the ages, many visitors coming to the enormous sandstones have wanted to leave their "mark," using a hammer and chisel while marring the natural beauty of the rocks.

The most elaborate and famous graffito is the John W. Larson 1921 handiwork mentioned above, but there are many others as well, and together, they make this one of the most interesting and beguiling rock formations I have ever found in Pennsylvania.

For instance, here can be found the silhouette of a woman's head, which is thought to have been created by a female carver sometime after the Larson map. It has an interesting history, for upon closer inspection, there is revealed an image of a lone wolf, supposedly added by her lonely husband after she died during surgery in 1962.

Another silhouette on a different rock is just a mere outline, a single feather on its head identifying it as that of an American Indian.

---

5. T. L Wall, *Clearfield County Pa. Present and Past*, 35-36.
6. D. S. Maynard, *Historical View of Clinton County*, 153.

A large carving of a hand with some missing fingers and pointing to the right, also believed to be completed by John W. Larson, still can be seen on a boulder along the Bilger's Rocks Trail today.

This chapter includes photos of some of the unique carvings and other spots that can be found at Bilger's rocks. The author took them in April of 2021 during a tortuous hike through the rocks, with squeezes through tight crevices and cautious steps over fissures extending thirty feet into the ground! But the soothing sound of Bilger's Run, with its numerous small waterfalls bubbling over the rocks, was a calming influence, as was the desire to see the next natural landmark.

I'm indebted to William M. Ammerman of Clearfield, who, as the official Bilger's Rocks Association tour guide, led me through the rocks to its significant rooms and carvings and regaled me with the stories about them that have been passed down through the ages.

LOCATION: Bilger's Rocks is a park in Clearfield County, near Grampian in Bloom Township (DD GPS Coordinates: 40.9939479, -78.5922485). From the County Seat of Clearfield County, follow Route 322 west and take the Route 219 exit. Follow Route 219 south. After passing Coffee Road on the left, look for Bilger's Rocks Road on the left. Follow this road for several miles until you see the parking area and park on the left.

CHAPTER 8

THE OLD IMPROVEMENT

Although there is an air of mystery that surrounds many of the out-of-the-way mountain landmarks that are highlighted in this book, the puzzling structures that can be seen on top of Nittany Mountain just east of the town of Centre Hall present an enigma that is more confounding and mysterious than most other mountain landmarks that can be found in Pennsylvania.

Of course, the stone towers on Nittany Mountain mentioned in the chapter titled "Castles in the Air" are just as mystifying to those who stumble upon them for the first time and do not know about their origins. But in that case, we know who built those towers, why he did so, and when. However, we cannot say the same about the structures on that mountain to the east.

Descriptions of the odd formations that could be found here fired my imagination and that of my young friends when we were teenagers growing up in Centre Hall and looking for adventure. The older boys who told us about it called the place "Council Rocks" and said it had been a place of Indian campfires, which made it even more mysterious and which drew us even more strongly to its heights. And it was many years later, when I was collecting stories for my Pennsylvania Fireside Tales books, I learned that one of the theories as to how these manmade structures got here was that they were indeed built by Indians who once had a village on this site.

The story about those Indians and their supposed village here is the stuff of early romance novels and can be found in the chapter titled "Council

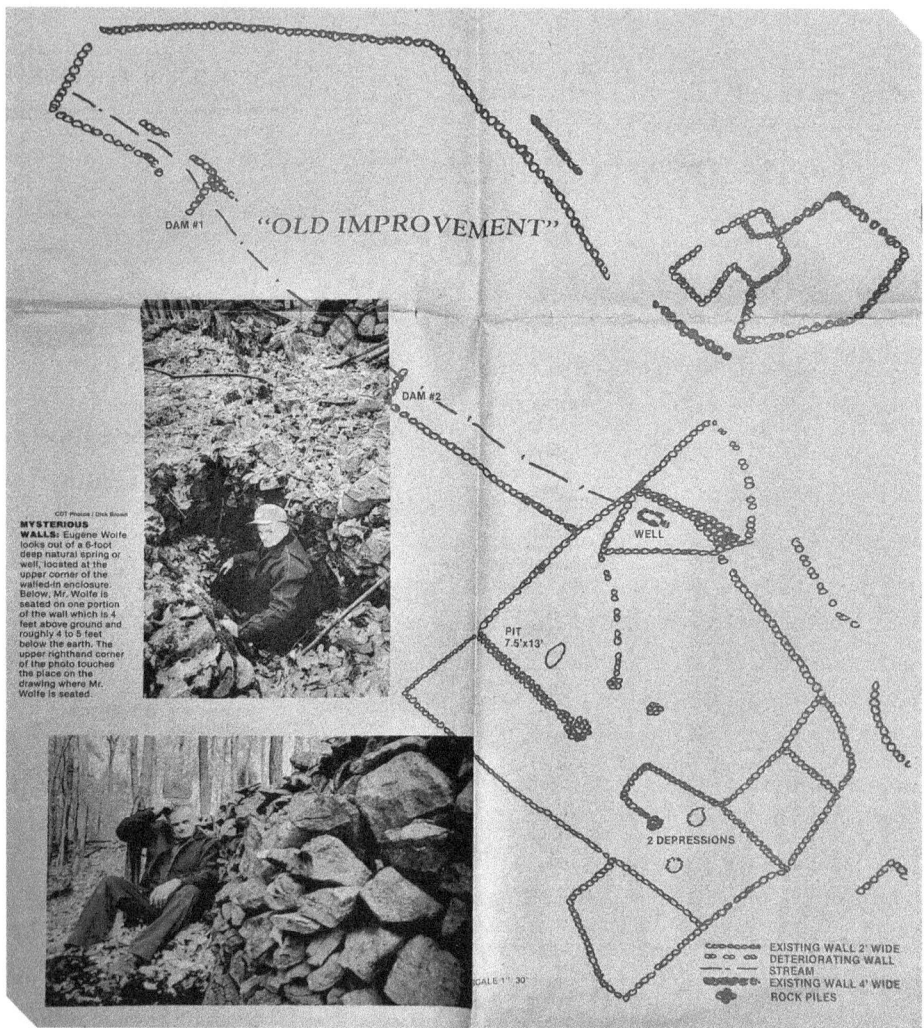

Diagram of the Old Improvement. Drawn by archeologists, it appeared in the *Centre Daily Times* of State College on November 6, 1983. The article, titled "Walls Refuse To Yield Their Secrets", included photos of the landowner of that time standing in the site's well and also sitting along one of the many rock walls whose origins remain a mystery even to this day.

Rocks" of my *Pennsylvania Fireside Tales Volume 4*. But despite its appeal and the possibility of it being true, there were, I was to learn, other theories as to who constructed the walls and cairns found here.

Another of those explanations is also based on the times when Native Americans still held some sway over the land, and this tale claims that early settlers built the enclosures found on the mountaintop to hide their livestock when Indian war parties were expected to swoop down on local settlements. And yet another theory states that an old hermit who lived here laid up the stone walls and cairns to pass the time.

Then there was a story put out by "fake-lorist" Henry W. Shoemaker in which he claimed the stone walls at the site are the remains of paddocks built as enclosures for thoroughbred horses that John Morton, a signer of the Declaration of Independence, wanted to raise and breed here.[1] A Centre County historian easily debunked that notion by studying land records and proving that of all the owners of this mountain ground, starting with General James Potter, none were named John Morton.[2]

These stories and the mystery surrounding the site eventually attracted the interest of archeologists, and in 1959 and again in 1983, several of them inspected the 15-acre site. Excavations were done in numerous spots, and under one cairn, the archeologists found evidence of what appeared to be a burial mound, but later analysis concluded the bones found there were those of animals.[3]

Digging was also done along two of the rock walls, which still extended three feet above the forest floor, and to everyone's surprise, the walls extended five feet into the ground, making their initial height eight feet. The fact that the walls were so deeply entrenched made it obvious that they were extremely old, that it must have taken many centuries for decaying leaf and plant matter to build up so high around them.[4]

Despite further work, the scientists were left with no solution as to who might have constructed the walls and cairns or why; they found no clues to shed any light on the old mystery that had perplexed local landowners for several hundred years.[5] They could only make some educated guesses, with one noting that stacking rocks over colonial graves was common to prevent disinterment by wild animals. Others noted that Indians did build cairns to either honor their dead or to mark paths through the dense forests of the

---

1. Henry W. Shoemaker, "Stone Fences are Centre County Oddity, Folklorist Points Out," *Centre County Heritage*, Vol. 8, No. 2, Oct. 1972, publication of Centre County Historical Society of State College, Pa.
2. Barbara Bruggebors, "Walls Refuse To Yield Their Secrets," newspaper article appearing November 6, 1983, in the *Centre Daily Times* of State College, Pa.
3. Ibid.
4. Ibid.
5. "Wolfe's wall still mystifies architects," an article appearing June 25, 1985, in the *Centre Daily Times* of State College, Pa.

Photo of another rock wall at the Old Improvement, 1983.

colonial period. It was also noted that stone piles were often created as the result of colonial field clearance.[6]

But although these ideas might explain the presence of stone cairns found at the Old Improvement site, they do not account for the extensive stone walls that were not just randomly thrown together but carefully laid in place at this same spot. So, the question remained unanswered, and no further archeological work seems to have been done to solve it. Nonetheless, it turned out that the site is not unique, which may provide further clues as to its origin or further complicate the mystery surrounding it.

Several other places in Pennsylvania have sites with arrays of stone structures similar to those on Nittany Mountain. Stone cairns built by parties unknown have been found in the mountains of Pennsylvania's Clinton and Montour Counties, and there are probably other places like them that lie hidden in other out-of-the-way and inaccessible places throughout the state. There are two in particular, however, that have been discovered and are of particular note because of their impressive size and design. In

---

6. Salvatore Trento, *The Search For Lost America*, 32.

THE OLD IMPROVEMENT

View of the Old Improvement site and walls today, 2021.

Another view of the Old Improvement site and walls today, 2021.

One of the last Old Improvement walls, 2021.

both those cases, the origins of the constructions are, like those on Nittany Mountain, puzzles wrapped in an enigma.

Said to be the most extensive site of this kind in Pennsylvania, the stone cairns in Susquehanna County's Endless Mountains are located along Hop Bottom Creek east of Montrose in the Poconos vacation paradise. This was an area once extensively populated by Native Americans, and so the stone structures were originally thought to have been constructed by them. But why they built so many in the same spot still left many wondering whether Indians built them.[7]

Likewise, in the Oley Hills of Berks County, there is a 46-acre site of winding stone walls, huge cairns, and stone piles thought by some to resemble human or animal forms. Here, once again, scholars have decided the constructions are of Native American origin, probably built for ceremonial or hunting purposes, but those opinions are still inconclusive and cannot be accepted until further technological tests can be completed.[8]

See the chapter titled "Mysteries in Stone" in this volume for more details about the Oley Hills and Susquehanna County sites and other similar sites, but also realize that such cairn sites are not unique to Pennsylvania. They have been discovered in Alabama, Arizona, Illinois, Missouri, New Jersey, New Mexico, Ohio, Tennessee, New York, West Virginia, and most New England states. But only Illinois, New York, Ohio, Tennessee, and West Virginia sites have stone walls. And besides the Old Improvement, there is only one other cairn site in Pennsylvania with stone walls: that of the Oley Hills in Berks County.[9]

So it seems apparent that these places of seemingly unsolvable mystery have the primary feature of stone cairns, stone walls, or both. However, they also are similar in other ways that may lead to an explanation as to who built them. To get there, we should first list the similarities in question. Those who have cataloged the sites have noted the following interesting features:

1. They are usually found on the upward eastside slopes of hills and mountains.
2. Walls are of dry stone construction and can be six feet high.
3. A water source such as a stream, lake, or river is found nearby.
4. All sites where archeological excavations have been done have revealed no evidence suggesting they are burial sites, but they were used for ancient ceremonialism.[10]

---

7. "The mysterious stone cairns of Susquehanna County," February 14, 2010 article found on www.adverbly.net.
8. Michael Yoder, "Old stone cairns of northern Berks County and southern Lehigh County are a mystery," the *Reading Eagle*, May 25, 2016.
9. Trento, *op. cit.*, 225-243.
10. Ibid, *op. cit.*, 32.

These features all correspond to those found at the Old Improvement site, which are as follows:

1. It is located near the mountaintop on an upward eastern slope.
2. Archeological excavations have shown that the walls were eight feet high when first built.
3. A small stream flows down the mountainside nearby.
4. Archeological excavations have not uncovered any evidence that it is a burial site.
5. Burnt animal bones excavated by archeologists may indicate some form of ceremonial rites once occurred at this spot.

As noted earlier in this chapter, many ideas have been put forth about the builders of such places, including one that suggests they were built in pre-Columbian times when ancient Phoenician sailors came here in the Bronze Age to mine for copper and tin. Evidence of such mining has been

The old well today, and the stone circle around it, 2021.

More of the remaining Old Improvement walls, 2021.

Close-up of the same wall, 2021.

found at these places in some cases, but it seems to stretch the imagination too far when it's considered how widespread the sites are and how daunting and laborious it would have been to transport excavated minerals to seaports for shipping them back across the Atlantic Ocean.[11]

Perhaps it's a mystery that will never be solved, one that is, in fact, unsolvable. And that seems to become more and more probable as the years go by. These sites are not immortal and will eventually disappear as nature tears them down and covers them up.

Much to my dismay, this eventuality was brought starkly to my attention when I revisited the Old Improvement in the spring of 2021, almost forty years after my first visit in the 1980s. On my first visit here, I could see numerous stone walls, some at least three feet high, snaking all over the mountainside, and I also found the top of a deep well that had once been dug there.

But on my visit in 2021, I was disappointed to find that many of the walls were no longer visible, and of those that could be seen, only a foot or two remained above ground. Even the well had caved in and was now no more than a small depression in the forest floor. It seemed like a part of local history had been lost forever and perhaps a part of human history. I walked back down the mountainside, wondering if the spirits of those who had built the walls had also finally deserted the place.

> **LOCATION: The Old Improvement** rock site is located on the summit of Nittany Mountain east of Centre Hall (DD GPS (approx.) Coordinates: 40.8903, -77.6275). From the traffic light in Centre Hall, head east on Route 192. In two to three miles is a farm on the left with a green-roofed silo. From a field beside that farmstead, you can follow a mountain stream to the mountaintop and the rock city. Permission from the farmer is required.

---

11. Ibid, *op. cit.*, 26, 29, 192, 199-202.

CHAPTER 9

SATAN'S HANDIWORK

A farmer's life has never been an easy one, but when the earliest settlers came to Pennsylvania to make a new life for themselves, they not only faced the unending tasks faced by those who farm, but they also had the formidable chore of first having to clear patches of ground to plant their crops.

That job must have seemed impossible, given the enormous size of the trees that towered over them and which had grown to such heights that they would have rivaled the Gigantes, that race of giants celebrated in Greek mythology. The vastness of the forest must have been formidable as well, as settlers in northeastern Pennsylvania called those mountains "The Endless Mountains," a name assigned to them by the Delaware Indians[1] and indicative of the awe in which they were held. It is a title still used today to refer to that same region. But determination and hard work ruled the day, and by tree girdling, brush burning, and following that adage of "many hands make light work," they turned their tasks into excuses for social gatherings.

Many fine farms were hewn from the wilderness due to frolics like grubbing bees, log rolling venues, barn raisings, wood chopping contests, butcherings, and the like,[2] a practice still followed by the Amish sects in Pennsylvania today. The forest land on mountain tops was tackled first

---
1. D. C. Henning, "Tales of the Blue Mountains," *Journal of the Schuylkill County Historical Soc., Vol. IV*, No. 2, June, 1912, Pottsville, Pa., 125.
2. Whitcomb Fletcher Stevenson, *Pennsylvania Agriculture And Country Life, 1640-1840*, p. 439.

Satan's Handiwork in Tioga County. Taken in Tioga County in the early 1900s, this photo, appearing in the Ridgway Record at that time, shows a landscape that was typical of what remained after lumbering interests pillaged the land and left a barren and cheerless prospect behind. (Courtesy of Penna. State Archives, Public Relations Office, RG-6 Dept. of Forest and Waters.)

since the trees there were not as large as those on the bottom lands where the soil was more fertile and water sources more plentiful.

Those early pioneers regarded some of those larger trees with respect, calling the largest ones "Old Settlers" and using them as landmark references to guide others.[3] But the forest where these monarchs reigned could be just as daunting as one traveler through the primeval forests of western Pennsylvania found out in 1798.

In his diary, kept during his journey, Joshua Sharpless noted that, after reaching the end of a cleared road, "we entered the wilderness without any path. A number of trees, being marked last fall, were now to be our guides. It was a thick woods we had to pass through, with a great quantity of young stuff and brush in the way."[4]

The passage was plagued by some other obstacles like continual successions of logs to cross, jumbles of large stones and rocks, almost perpendicular

---

3. Arch Bristow, *Old Time Tales of Warren County*, 114.
4. Ibid., 376-377.

Rothrock's "Pennsylvania desert." As it appeared along Lick Run, near the Village of Cross Fork, Potter County, in the early 1900's. (Photo by W. T. Clark. Courtesy of Penna. State Archives, Public Relations Office, RG-6 Dept. of Forest and Waters.)

descents into swamps, and such a thick interlacing of pine and hemlock tree roots on the ground that travel was slowed considerably by them. Underbrush and low-hanging tree limbs also proved troublesome,[5] and so it was little wonder that people of that period did not begrudge the work and time it took to establish better roadways and clear fields for planting crops.

But another obstacle that often made clearing mountaintop fields and roads even more difficult was the presence of the vast boulder fields and enormous rock cities that seemed to have sprouted up on their own at the higher elevations. They were not only a deterrence to transportation and farming, but the rock impediments also presented a mystery to those who encountered them.

Perhaps it was the dim twilight with its greenish mist that was characteristic of the primeval forest, even in midday, or maybe it was the eerie sounds of the wilderness, including the soft lamentations of mourning doves, or the haunting, almost otherworldly cries of the woods thrush, that evoked superstitious sentiments in the minds of the forest dwellers of that

---

5. Ibid.

time and led them to their conclusions about the many rock obstacles that stood in their way.

And the complete lack of light in the thickest parts of the forest could also have contributed to unearthly thoughts as well, such as the dismal section experienced by Bishop Gottlieb Spangenberg when traveling along the Sheshequin Indian Path through present-day Lycoming County in 1745.

"This is a wilderness," wrote Spangenberg, "where one does not see the sun all day. The woods are so thickly grown that sometimes one can hardly see twenty paces ahead."[6]

Such conditions are likely to invoke gloomy and depressing thoughts in even the most sanguine minds, and such impressions might have led some of the state's earliest pioneers to wonder why the Almighty would have allowed potential cropland to be rendered unusable by covering it with seemingly immovable boulders and ledges of solid rock.

Sorely-tried minds could then have arrived at the only reasonable explanation: that it was the work of the Devil. After all, Satan's sole purpose seemed to be to find ways to defy God by tormenting his creations in any way he could, and what better way to accomplish that than to frustrate mankind's attempts to feed themselves by blocking their means of doing so?

These convictions could only have been hardened by the harshness of the life the frontiersmen endured, which did not get any easier as decades passed, particularly during Pennsylvania's lumbering era, when men of strong constitution were required to endure the harsh and dangerous working conditions in the primeval forests. One such man was Hiram Cranmer, born in Hammersley Fork of Clinton County in 1891 and who, by his admission, "learned to ride a floating log at the age of seven."[7]

Cranmer was a veteran of the First World War, serving with Battery B, 321st Pennsylvania Field Artillery, and surviving a poisonous gas attack during the Battle of the Argonne Forest in 1918. Before going off to The Great War, and for some years after returning, he worked for several logging companies in north central Pennsylvania, recalling some of

---

6. Paul A. W. Wallace, *Indian Paths of Pennsylvania*, 6.
7. Thomas R. Cox, editor, "Harvesting the Hemlock: the Reminiscences of a Pennsylvania Wood-hick," *Pennsylvania History*, Vol. 51, no. 2, April 1984, 122.

those experiences in a series of articles on the history of lumbering, which appeared in the *Lock Haven Express* during April and May of 1948.[8] One of those articles, which recalls his eyewitness account of a man drowning during a log jam, shows how devilishly dangerous the logging profession could be: "I watched a man drown on a log drive. While breaking a "center jam," a man fell in, and while the bateau was rescuing him, four men were forced to ride the logs. The man drowned. Frank Lynch led the men. He lost his nerve in trying to get on another center jam and fell in. He came up a hundred feet below the jam. Instead of wading to his left ashore, he waded down the stream for a hundred and fifty yards, to his shoulders in water, shouted several times, waded among the logs and went under them. His body was found downstream, six miles from where he drowned. In his pockets were seven cents, a piece of chewing tobacco and a helgramite [aquatic larvae of a winged insect often found on or under submerged rocks]. Twenty minutes after he went to work, he was under the logs."[9]

The harshness of life in the first centuries of Pennsylvania's history and the natural obstacles encountered in trying to improve their lives could have colored the thoughts of those who had to cope with those harsh realities. It seems that it could have even led some of them when they encountered the rock barriers on the mountaintops they were trying to clear for fields or roads, to name those obstructions for their supposed evil creator.

In the end, however, in the late nineteenth and early twentieth century, after the lumber companies were finished cutting down millions of the trees that once stood in the state's vast forests, the denuded slopes they left behind looked like a desolate and dismal desert. And as forest fire after forest fire swept through the abandoned brush piles, shattered stumps, and dense thickets of briar, sumac, and scrub oak, nothing was left but scorched and blackened earth, best described as nothing less than another example of Satan's handiwork.

Such practices and the devastation they created led Joseph T. Rothrock (see the chapter titled "Rothrock's Rock" in this volume), Pennsylvania's first state forester, to describe the deplorable conditions as the "Pennsylvania

---

8. Ibid.
9. Ibid.

"After the Lumbermen." Photo taken by J. T. Rothrock in Bear Meadows of Centre County about 1910. His added notation: "Such waste is an invitation to the forest fire". (Courtesy of Penna. State Archives, Public Relations Office, RG-6 Dept. of Forest and Waters.

Desert,"[10] and prompted him and other conservationists to create a state Forestry Commission, eventually preserving over four million acres of state-owned forest reserves.

---

10. Elizabeth H. Thomas, "Forest Protection and the Founding of Pennsylvania's First Forestry School, 1901-1903," *Pennsylvania History*, Vol. 44, no. 4, October 1977, 292.

The "Wolf Oak," Rhonymeade Farm, Centre County, 2021. This old veteran once served as a boundary marker on the corner of two adjacent properties. Foresters condemn barely-surviving trees like this as worthless space fillers and refer to them as "wolf" trees, but these forest old-timers serve as a valuable habitat for numerous creatures of the forest.

In his lectures and writings, Rothrock often recalled dense green cathedrals of beech, yellow birch, sugar maple, white pine and hemlock comprised the Pennsylvania forest of his youth, and he lamented its destruction. It was hard for him, and many others, to believe that all that forest was gone, along with the huge monarchs that seemed invincible due to their mammoth size.

Among those giants was a huge white pine in Highland Township of Elk County. Felled by the lumberman's ax on lands of the Central Pennsylvania Lumber Company, a picture of the stump left behind appeared in another issue of The Ridgway Record in 1910, and the caption described it as measuring 26 feet 10 inches in circumference! Other titans like this one were sometimes left standing because they were boundary markers or on land whose ownership was questioned. An example of one such giant is a gnarled tree with massive spreading branches that still stands today on the Rhonymeade Farm conservation property in Centre County.

Known as the "wolf" oak, this specimen appears to be a survivor from a much earlier time, and the nearby, clearly discerned tracks of an old stagecoach road lends credence to that assumption.

LOCATION: Rhonymeade Farm is in Potter Township near Centre Hall, Centre County (DD GPS Coordinates: 40.808889, -77.721111). Take Route 45 west (Earlystown Road) at the traffic light intersection of Routes 45 and 144 south of Centre Hall. Follow 45 west, approximately 2 miles to Rimmey Road on the right. Turn onto Rimmey Road and follow the sign to Rhonymeade at the top of the hill.

CHAPTER 10

MYSTERIES IN STONE

In our chapter titled "The Old Improvement," there is a discussion regarding unusual stone structures that can be found on Nittany Mountain of Centre County. In that chapter, there are references to unusual stone cairns in Berks and Susquehanna Counties, whose origins are steeped in as much mystery as that of the unusual rock formations on Nittany Mountain. In this chapter, we'll delve more closely into the Berks and Susquehanna sites and reveal another site in Clinton County, whose cairns are a noted landmark on a remote mountaintop surrounded by an untamed forest of vast proportions.

The Clinton County cairns can be found in Colebrook Township of that county, but they are not readily accessible. Those who wish to find them will find themselves challenged by a strenuous hike along a rugged state forest road that extends through State Game Lands #89 near the small village of Farrandsville. The cairns lie within a remote wilderness formed by Sproul State Forest and Bucktail State Park Natural Area, where there are many miles to wander, presenting the hiker with beautiful natural wonders to appreciate and places showing traces of human intervention whose origins have long been forgotten.

Lumbermen who have conducted lumbering operations here say that they have no idea who might have built the Colebrook cairns, as they are often referred to, but that this same place was once a haven for "moonshiners," evidence of their moonshine stills being found by those same lumbermen when they harvested the timber off the area.[1]

---
1. James Maguire, interviewed February 14, 2021.

Overview of the three Colebrook cairns in Clinton County.

The idea that this spot was once the center for the production of distilled spirits and so once reeked of the strong smells of moonshine is supported by topographical maps of the area, which show that the creek that runs through Sproul State Forest near here is called Whisky Run, which flows into Lick Run near Farrandsville. But the lumbermen did not believe that the "moonshiners" would have taken the time to build the stone cairns at this same spot, suggesting that, like themselves, they probably "had better and more profitable things to do with their time."[2]

There are four other theories as to who might have stacked the rocks into the complex towers that stand here, including the idea that it could have been farmers clearing their fields, members of the Civilian Conservation Corp who cleared the Hazard Road, the forestry road through here, and whose camp was nearby; pre-Columbian explorers marking trails or creating ceremonial spots; or Native Americans who built them for that same purpose—a theory that has led some to call the sites "Ceremonial

---

2. Ibid.

Close-up view of one of the taller cairns at the Colebrook cairns in Clinton County. (Photo courtesy of Lou Bernard.)

stone Landscapes."[3] Each theory seems to have possible merits and may hold the final answer to the mystery.

Just like the lumberman, it would seem that farmers would have spent their time more profitably than by carefully piling up stone towers and cairns, and there is no evidence that they ever did create such structures. It is far more likely that they would have carted stones surfacing or plowed up in their fields onto a large stone pile in nearby woods or at the edge of the field. Such stone piles are often seen next to farmers' fields and are just that: piles of stones thrown onto a heap with no well-planned design or evident architectural characteristics that make them stand out in any way.

The suggestion that the stone cairn structures are the results of efforts of CCC camp workers seems plausible in the case of the Colebrook cairns, given that a CCC camp was located nearby and its men did much work in

---

3. See "Native American Ceremonial Stone Landscape Sites in the Northeast" on the Native American Roots website at http://nativeamericannetroots.net/diary/1973. Also see James E. Gage, "A Walk in the Woods - Exploring Stone Cairns and Stone Piles," Submitted On March 31, 2008 https://EzineArticles.com/expert/James_E._Gage/188583.

Tallest cairn at the Colebrook cairns in Clinton County.

the area. Also supporting this idea is the resemblance of the conical cairn found at the Colebrook site to the conical "upper springhouse" cairn built by members of CCC camp S-135, which was located along present-day State Route 44 in Potter County.

Another theory that's been proposed for the origins of the stone cairns is that European seafarers, arriving in North America before it was "discovered" by Christopher Columbus, built these places. However, there is no historical evidence to support this conjecture nor any apparent explanation as to why such adventurers might have expended the considerable effort it would have taken to erect the cairns (once again, see the chapter in this volume titled "The Old Improvement" for more on this subject).

Then there's the idea that Native Americans were the architects and builders of the Colebrook stone structures long before white men came along and took this land for their own. There are other cairn sites just like this in Pennsylvania and other states, and although they are also thought to have been built by Indians before the white man's arrival upon the

The conical cairn and its viewing port, Colebrook Cairns, Clinton County.

continent, no one knows for sure if they did so or even why. It's a debate that's been simmering for decades, and it's generally conceded now that further evidence is needed before a definitive answer is reached.

The puzzling thing about some of the most spectacular cairn sites is the number of cairns clustered within a small area. This configuration is not consistent with anything white men would ever need to do, and so it's believed by many that these places are remnants of Native American ceremonial sites—"a place where Native Americans came to pray, hold ceremonies, and practice their religion."[4]

Of the four possible theories that have been brought forth to identify the builders of the cairns at these places, it seems none have enough evidence to award them the distinction of having the final say in the matter. Depending on the site, one theory would seem to fit better, but one alone does not. However, the cairn sites in Berks and Susquehanna Counties provide ample evidence for those favoring the Native American proposal.

These two places are the largest and most impressive in Pennsylvania, rivaling the most spectacular cairn sites in other states. The Oley Hills site,

---
4. Ibid.

The upper springhouse at CCC camp S-135. (Photo courtesy of Curt Weinhold.)

for example, covers an area of almost fifty acres where meandering dry stone walls and numerous groups of cairns seem to appear in every clearing and on every sun-dappled knoll.

Perhaps the other-worldly atmosphere of the rock formations and the unsolved mysteries they hold affect visitors' imaginations. Many have claimed that they can discern animal or human shapes formed by the rock piles that dot the Oley Hills. Furthermore, those who have studied the formations in great detail have concluded the cairns were built with intentional celestial alignments and exhibit other characteristics of intelligent design.

The same might be said of the 120 Susquehanna cairns along Hop Bottom Creek near Montrose in Susquehanna County. Here, just like the cluster on the Oley Hills, the number of cairns concentrated together seems to indicate they served as a ceremonial site, and from the lack of historical and archeological evidence suggesting otherwise, the most likely builders seem to have been Native Americans.

That this might be a possibility is no doubt a hard fact for historians to accept. Fifty years ago, a respected authority on Pennsylvania's Native

Americans stated, "The Indians of Pennsylvania have left no monuments in stone like the palaces and temples of the Mayas and Aztecs, which today make their ruined cities look amazing even in an age of engineering marvels."[5]

As noted previously, however, further evidence is needed to reach such a conclusion. However, pictures taken at the Oley Hills and Susquehanna cairn sites offer the reader some evidence they can use to form their conclusions.

The picture of the "turtle" cairn in the Oley Hills is particularly interesting. The large boulders on the left and right in this formation are thought by some to represent the turtle's head and legs, with the stone cairn representing its shell. If true, then it might be strong evidence of Native American design since in the folklore of many Native American tribes, including the *Lenni Lenape* Indians, who were the original inhabitants of Berks County, turtles played a prominent role, especially in their creation myths.[6]

Afterthought: Some 75 years ago, another mystery regarding "a massive stonework of great antiquity existing in the Allegheny Mountains of Centre County" came to light via an early 1880s account published in the *Philadelphia Times*. Therein, the reporter described this marvelous rock assembly as "probably the most remarkable pre-historic fortification in the United States," also claiming that the structure supposedly consisted of a "semicircular wall, possibly 800 feet in diameter," which burrowed into the mountainside near the headwaters of Moshannon Creek.

The wall rose to eight feet and was held in place by "cement of a curious composition unknown to local chemists." The site was also said to be marked by six to eight stone pillars, "some of them being from six to eight feet high, and "evidently used as altars in some forgotten age."

The only problem was that when curious historians attempted to find the spot, they could not, even after asking locals about its whereabouts. They all reluctantly abandoned further efforts to find it "until later, in the

---

5. Paul A. W. Wallace, *op. cit.*, 1.
6. See "Native American Turtle Mythology" on the Native Languages of America website at www.native-languages.org/legends-turtle.htm.

Cairn stacked on boulder platform. (Cairn field near Montrose, Susquehanna County: Photograph © Brian A. Morganti / www.stormeffects.com.)

Hillside cairn field with boulder bases. (Cairn field near Montrose, Susquehanna County: Photograph © Brian A. Morganti / www.stormeffects.com.)

MYSTERIES IN STONE

Flat-topped conical and beehive cairns. (Cairn field near Montrose, Susquehanna County: Photograph © Brian A. Morganti / www.stormeffects.com.

Conical and columnar cairn field - View 2. (Cairn field near Montrose, Susquehanna County: Photograph © Brian A. Morganti / www.stormeffects.com.

The "turtle" cairn at Oley Hills. (Attribution: By en:User:Geophile took this picture on site - en:File:Oley hills cairns sm.jpg, CC BY-SA 3.0, https://en.wikipedia.org/w/index.php?curid=13459123.)

hope that reliable information would be forthcoming in the meantime."[7] To this day, it has never been found, leading some to suggest that it was a story concocted by the Philadelphia reporter to increase newspaper sales and further his reputation.

---

7. Albert Rung, *Rung's Chronicles of PA History*, article dated 3 August 1946, and titled "Ancient Stone Work in Centre County." See pp 32-33.

LOCATIONS:

Farrandsville Cairns: The cairns are located along the Hazard Road in State Game Lands #89 in Sproul State Forest near the town of Farrandsville, in Colebrook Township of Clinton County (DD GPS Coordinates: 41.185067, -7751165). Drive through Lock Haven, cross the Jay Street Bridge, and west to Farrandsville. Drive through Farrandsville to its end and park near the ruins of CCC Camp S-135. From there, follow the steep and rocky Hazard Road for about a mile, and when you reach Game Plot #4 on the left, hike back the forest road beside it to the cairns.

CCC Camp S-135: The site of this former Civilian Conservation Corp Camp is located along State Route #44 in Potter County (DD GPS Coordinates: 41.519367, -77622883). See the previous paragraph.

Montrose Cairns is located on private land along Hop Bottom Creek near Montrose, Susquehanna County (DD GPS Coordinates: 41.713684, -75699128). From Montrose, follow Route 29 north, then turn right onto Route 167 east/south. Follow Route 167 until you can turn left onto Township Road 2015. The cairn fields are hidden in a wooded area on the left after one to two miles. They are on private land, and no trespassing is allowed.

Oley Hills Cairn field: This site is also on private land in the Oley Hills of Berks County southeast of Kutztown and along the former Oley and Perkiomen-Lehigh Indian Paths (DD GPS Coordinates: 40.495, -75654). From Kutztown, follow US Route 222 east, then turn right and head south on Farmington Road. At a T intersection, turn left onto State Street and follow it into the village of Longswamp. At Longswamp, turn left onto Clay Road at the intersection of Longswamp Road and Clay Road (Longswamp Road turns into Hidden Valley Road at the intersection). The cairn fields are to the southeast of the intersection and on private land, with no trespassing allowed.

CHAPTER 11

PENNSYLVANIA'S GRAND CANYON

The Pine Creek Gorge is possibly one of our state's most impressive tourist attractions. Otherwise known as the Grand Canyon of Pennsylvania, it is almost fifty miles long and 1500 feet deep at its deepest point. Beginning at Ansonia in Tioga County, the gorge ends below Waterville in Lycoming County. Geologists say the declivity was formed over 350 million years ago through the combined action of glaciers and erosion by Pine Creek.

Today, there are two state parks along the canyon rim where tourists can enjoy spectacular views of this natural wonder and the surrounding mountains: Leonard Harrison and Colton Point State Parks. The unusual topography here was also a source of amazement to the local Indians, and some think they had their version of how it was created. According to those sources, the aborigines believed the canyon was a special creation of their Great Spirit, who dug it out with his tomahawk, but others believe this tale is misplaced, including a Potter County farmer who told us an even more interesting legend about the canyon when we interviewed him in 1989.

"Dug it out with a hatchet?" he queried. "That's possible, but I thought that was over there at Wyalusing Rocks where the Great Spirit took the tomahawk and chopped the mountain off. I didn't hear it about the Grand Canyon. I thought I heard it about the Wyalusing Rocks on the

The covered wagons in the Grand Canyon. With the Percheron and Belgian two-horse teams that pull the wagons along the rail trail once used by the Jersey Shore, Pine Creek, and Buffalo Railway Company to transport logs out of the canyon. The last train traveled through here in 1988, and the tracks were subsequently removed, leaving the rail bed which was converted to the present-day rail trail.

Susquehanna. I heard that years ago from the old-timers over there."[1] (See the chapter titled "Native American Mementoes" in Volume 2 for more about Wyalusing Rocks)

Although there is confusion about at least one of the canyon's legends, there's no doubt that Indians once frequented this area. History states that they even had a path that ran the entire length of the great gorge, a wilderness trail the early settlers here named the Pine Creek Path.[2] The well-worn warriors' path connected present-day Jersey Shore with Ansonia, and from there, it continued to the Genesee Valley of New York State. It was neither a route for the faint-hearted nor one a tenderfoot would have relished. Potter County farmers taking their grain to mills in Jersey Shore used sturdy teams of oxen to pull their wagons over the route, knowing

---

1. Donald Heggenstaller, (born 1921), recorded November 16, 1989.
2. Paul A. W. Wallace, *Indian Paths of Pennsylvania*, 130.

that their horses were not strong enough to pull the heavier loads, mainly because there was no road.

"I crossed Pine Creek eighty times going to and eighty times coming from mill," wrote John Peet in describing his trip from Potter County to Jersey Shore via the Pine Creek Path in July of 1811. "I was gone eighteen days, broke two axletrees to my wagon, upset twice, and one wheel came off in crossing the creek."[3]

Although the hardiest and bravest settlers traveled through the canyon, some folks today contend that Indians may have avoided parts of it altogether, and they did so because they were afraid. The reason for that fear was explained to our Potter County farmer by an aged Seneca Indian who made annual visits to the ancestral home of his forebears. That same Potter County gentleman told it to me most engagingly and claimed he had experienced some of that same fear himself.

"Well, a lot of people say the Indians traveled the canyon, and they did not travel the canyon," claimed our Potter County farmer. "There was no way to get a boat up and down the canyon because of the log jams and the floods. And there was no way to get in and out of the canyon. The lumbermen had to clear the canyon from Blackwell's or Slate Run. Indians did not travel the canyon, regardless of what anybody said!

"There was only two crossings in the canyon. One was at Tiadaghton; the other one was clear down at Blackwells on the canyon. Now, the main trail, if I understand it right, is what the settlers followed. That would be from Tioga to Wellsboro and around by Marsh Creek and up Pine Creek, come around Ansonia, where Highway Six is today. That was the main trail, but there was a crossing in the canyon. The place where they could cross was at Tiadaghton.

"Now we live at the 'place of seven springs,' and this old fella, years ago, used to come through here about once a year. I can't tell you what his name was anymore, something like *Nay-My-Oh;* and he was of the Seneca tribe, out of Seneca, New York, and this was the place of his ancestors. He said the Senecas traveled through here—the warpath. It's on the north and south route of the Senecas to the Delawares and out over the Algerines to

---

3. Ibid.

Barbour's Rock. Once the shelter for Samuel Barbour, whose job was to break up log jams, using cant hooks or dynamite, in the Owassee Rapids of Pine Creek below. It was a dangerous job and Barbour died during one such attempt in the 1890's. This rocky and thickly-wooded cliff looks very similar to the cliff of the wailing child at Bradley Wales Lookout.

Slate Run on the way to the trading post at Tiadaghton. They went down towards Pine Mountain, where the warpath went.

"Over there right below Bradley Wales Lookout, there was a story that the Indians would not go into the canyon; would not cross anyplace there in the canyon because of that wailing child. According to what the old Seneca told me, the Senecas sacrificed a child from an unwed mother, what we would call a bastard child, for to get it to rain. The legend had it that they had throwed a child off of that cliff, and the child screamed all the way to the bottom. They figured if they would do that, it would change the weather because, for three years, there had been no rain. It didn't rain for three years—that many 'moons.'

"Well, the main drought, according to records—now we gotta go way back. The three years of no rain was back in the early 1600's. There's definite proof; up here in our forest museum, we've even got records of it. You often wonder why there was no trees that they ever cut, according to the lumber mill records, which was over two hundred years old.

"Now, according to the records of the sawmills, late 1800s, early 1900s, they have never cut any amount of trees that was over one-hundred and fifty years old. So if you go by that, and their records of the three years of no rain and the big fires, the "Big Burn" is what the Indians call it, why you can understand why there was only a few trees around that was over that age.

"There had been no rain this far in this part of the state. The big fires had wiped out all the game as well as all the forest, and there had been no rain for three years. They thought by taking this bastard child, we would call it, and sacrificing it to the rain god, they would get rain. And after that, because of the crying of the child, the Indians would never go to that place in the canyon; they would not cross there at Tiadaghton. Know what that sound is?

"You go to Bradley Wales Lookout and walk down to the far end of it, the south end, and you will see it. The Bradley Wales farmers up there they used that trail to go down the Tiadaghton, and they have widened it out.

"Them farmers up on top there used that trail to go over to the railroad. You go down to Tiadaghton, up from Tiadaghton Park, which I think they've closed now. You know, they took the railroad track out of the canyon, but if you go to Tiadaghton and go up the canyon to where the old wagon road come off of Bradley Wales, and you set there in the evening when the wind and warm air in the canyon start to rise, why, you'll hear it!

"Just in the summer; that's the only time I know I ever heard it when we was in there fishing years ago. Yeah, why I think it's nothing but the wind going up through the rock on the sides of Bradley Wales. See, the cold air comes off the top of the mountain and sucks the warm air up over the canyon!"[4]

It was a fascinating narrative, this old Indian legend passed down by an ancient member of the Seneca Nation to a Potter County farmer living on the land of the Indian's ancestors. And it's understandable why the Indians attached a supernatural significance to the wailing wind at Bradley Wales, especially to those who have heard it. Even though they know it's just the

---

4. Donald Heggenstaller, (born 1921), recorded November 16, 1989.

night wind, those who have experienced the sounds say they closely resemble a baby's cries. They are so realistic that our narrator recalled that when he first heard them, "it made the hairs stand up" on the back of his neck, and did so every time he subsequently heard them.[5]

Perhaps, then, given the reaction of modern-day folks, it seems likely that the same sounds did scare the less-sophisticated Indians of four hundred years ago; frightened them so badly that, just like the legend states, they did avoid this part of the canyon—this place they thought was haunted by the ghost of the wailing child. But has the legend survived to the twenty-first century, and can the sounds still be heard today? I decided there was no better way to find out than to take a trip through the canyon and discover the answers.

Much to my delight, I found that a picturesque trip through the canyon is offered today, and in a conveyance that not only takes the tourist through the canyon but also gives that same tourist a sense of what it was like for John Peet and other early settlers here, when they took their wagon trips up the Pine Creek Path.

The October wagon ride of several miles took us along the old rail trail that runs parallel to Pine Creek and spans 47 miles of the Pine Creek Gorge and beyond. Towering mountain peaks frowned down upon us, with their colorful autumn foliage reminding us that the cool clasp of winter was not that far away and their rocky slopes giving evidence as to how difficult it would be to make their ascent. Every now and then, our pleasurable journey was punctuated by the sights and sounds of mini-waterfalls cascading down rocky streambeds on those same hillsides.

But even though we could see that the canyon walls and the banks of Pine Creek are well-wooded and brush-covered today, that was not always the case. When lumber companies came here in the late 1880s, they aimed to harvest many of the magnificent virgin white pines and hemlocks that had grown here for centuries. The "lumber kings" had no respect for nature, conservation, or future generations, electing instead to clear-cut the forest along the entire canyon.

The result of such deplorable lumber harvests was the "Pennsylvania desert," which we addressed in our chapter titled "Satan's Handiwork"

---

5. Ibid.

Grand Canyon View, as seen from Bradley Wales Lookout in 1993, with the old railroad line rail bed visible on the canyon floor below and the cliff of the wailing child in the foreground.

in this volume. Along with that "desert" came the inevitable forest fires that blackened the earth and the disastrous erosion of land that was easily washed away because there was no longer any root system to hold it in place.

Fortunately, due to reclamation efforts by the Civilian Conservation Corps in the 1920s and 1930s, the forest was restored, and the mountains "bloomed" again. Even the whistle of the railroad engine could still be heard at that time, and it was a familiar sound throughout here up until the 1980s. But when the railroad finally shut down in the late 1980s, the whistles of the train engines fast became a distant memory. But one of the railroad's former employees seems determined that his memory should live on.

The tour guide told the story of the phantom track walker on our Conestoga wagon ride through the canyon in October 2021. He lives near Bradley Wales Lookout and claims that he often hears the sounds here that

Sweeping view of the Grand Canyon. Colton Point State Park as seen from the overlook at Leonard Harrison State Park.

resemble the cries of a wailing child. But his most interesting tale was of the strange light he often sees moving along the rail trail in the canyon floor just below the Bradley Wales Lookout.

The light resembles that of an old-time railroad lantern like the ones once carried by the "track walkers" hired by the railroad to inspect the tracks at night to ensure they were in good condition and not blocked by any major obstructions.

"I've tried to follow it," noted our storyteller, but you can never get to it. It always floats away whenever you get close to it. I heard the story from the old-timers here, who said it is the light from a railroad lantern carried by the last trackwalker who worked here and died of natural causes one night while walking along the tracks."[6]

If the ghostly lantern light tale has a basis, then the spirit who carries it has only partially succeeded in its bid for immortality. Today, no one

---

6. James Melko, interviewed October 7, 2021.

remembers his name, so he can only hope that his story lives on in the memories of locals and on the pages of this book.

Afterthought:
The Seneca legend about the sounds of the crying child in Pennsylvania's Grand Canyon may be dismissed by nay-sayers as fanciful story-telling. But even highly respected folklorists have realized that such stories ought not to be dismissed offhand. Or, as one of the most highly respected folklorists in this nation so aptly explained, "Historical facts may lie embedded in narratives filled with distorted and folkloristic elements." It is an opinion worth noting.[7]

That conclusion makes the Seneca legend of the wailing child even more intriguing. Not only does it suggest that the legend may be something of scholarly importance, but it also elevates it into the realm of the possible. Its historical details may have some truth behind them after all! That possibility, in turn, should increase the public's appreciation for one of Pennsylvania's greatest natural landmarks: the Pennsylvania Grand Canyon.

> **LOCATION:** Pennsylvania's Grand Canyon stretches from Ansonia in Tioga County to Waterville in Lycoming County (DD GPS Coordinates: 41.6967376, -77.451464). Its two state parks are most easily accessed from Wellsboro, Lycoming County, following Route 660 out of Wellsboro.

---

7. Richard M. Dorson, *American Folklore and the Historian*, 141.

CHAPTER 12

RATTLESNAKE ROCK
(Lycoming County)

That rattlesnakes were not only common in Pennsylvania at one time but also unbelievably numerous is a fact that cannot be disputed given the many historical accounts that describe the enormous clusters that could often be seen coiled up on rocks and stones to warm themselves in the sun. Even today, their numbers are surprisingly large, as seen by the quantities captured during the "Rattlesnake Roundups" that still, in 2023, take place in the counties of Potter, Cameron, Wyoming, and Bradford, and perhaps others too.

These events are "catch and release" captures without harming the snakes. The organizers of these events hope that the information they gain from the captured snakes will help them conserve the reptiles and their habitat. But what seems quite remarkable about these hunts is the number of snakes caught and the lengths of the largest ones, which often exceed four feet. It's also worth noting that the Pennsylvania Game Commission does sell licenses, so licensed hunters can kill one timber rattler a year, but the snake has to be at least 42 inches long!

Probably one of the first accounts describing the prevalence of rattlesnakes in Pennsylvania came from one Francois Michaux. In *Michaux's Travels to the West of the Allegheny Mountains*, he tells of encountering a man who had been bitten by a rattlesnake near Bedford in Bedford County in 1801. The man recovered, but Michaux noted that "there are a great many rattlesnakes in these mountainous parts of Pennsylvania; we found a

"Irvin George, Champion Snake Catcher of Perry County, 1921." (PA State Archives RG6.20: Department of Forests and Waters.)

great number of them killed upon the road. In the warm and dry season of the year, they come out from beneath the rocks, and inhabit those places where there is water."[1]

It was perhaps the subsequent historical descriptions of colossal rattlesnake congregations that gave free rein to the imaginations of tellers of tall tales, who, to create more interest in the books they wrote, shared descriptions of rattlesnakes that could have been taken from the books written by Baron Von Munchausen, a well-known late eighteenth-century narrator of false and highly-exaggerated exploits. Given some of the descriptions of Pennsylvania rattlesnakes found in early accounts written by some authors in that same period, it would seem Pennsylvania spawned some Munchausen's of its own.

One of the most lurid of those authors was British Author Thomas Ashe, who came to America in 1806 to explore and write about this new country that was so fascinating to his fellow Europeans. But it seemed

---

1. Francois Michaux, *Michaux's Travels*, 146.

"Irvin George Training His Snakes, 1921." (PA State Archives RG6.20, Department of Forests and Waters.)

when he picked up his pen, it ran away from him. For example, some of his descriptions of the wildlife he encountered in his American travels were obvious fabrications. Among the most egregious of those were his stories about killing a twelve-foot-long rattlesnake in Pennsylvania and shooting a bear with five-inch tusks and fifteen-inch long paws in that same state. He also claimed to have seen a twenty-foot-long alligator in Louisiana.[2]

Just as bombastic was Thomas Campanius Holm, who explored the Pennsylvania territory in the eighteenth century. "There is here," he writes, "a large and horrible serpent which is called a rattlesnake. It has a head like that of a dog and can bite off a man's leg as clear as it if had been

---

2. Thomas Ashe, *Travels in America*, p 14 (Volume 1, Letter 2), p 154 (Volume 2, Letter 15), p 343 (Volume 3, Letter 37).

hewn down with an axe . . . These snakes are three yards long and as thick as the thickest part of a man's leg. Their skins are much sought after by pregnant women; they tie them around their bodies and are quickly and easily delivered!"[3]

Another eighteenth-century writer, John David Schoepf, was just as outrageous in his claims about Pennsylvania rattlers, writing, "A rattlesnake of uncommon length was killed here in the year 1778 . . . . It was 18 feet long, and the stript skin measured two and a half feet in breadth."[4]

Perhaps these descriptions influenced a more well-known Pennsylvania writer, also known to be prone to exaggeration in his historical accounts. Philip Tome's vivid recollections of his hunting days are recalled in his self-published book *Pioneer Life, or Thirty Years a Hunter* (1854). There is no question that Tome's life in what was then the wilderness of northern Pennsylvania must have been somewhat comparable to that of such veteran frontiersmen like Daniel Boone or even Davy Crockett.

However, Tome's claim as to having seen the fabled "hoop snake," now largely discredited as nothing more than a product of someone's rich imagination, and of a deer that could not be shot, even at close range, cause doubts to be cast about his other observations as well, including those describing the prevalence of rattlesnakes in the northern tier counties of McKean, Potter, Elk, and Tioga during the mid-nineteenth century. And one of those observations concerns Rattlesnake Rock, the subject of this chapter.

Tome notes that when his parents first settled in the area, "the rattle-snakes were so numerous that we used to clear the yard and build fires around the house to keep them away." He also recalled, "On leaving the house, it was a necessary precaution for many years to put on a pair of woolen socks and leggings over our shoes to protect our legs from snakes."[5]

He goes on to write that the Pine Creek country at that time teemed with rattlesnakes from the mouth of Pine Creek and northward, there being six rattlesnake dens within a stretch of several miles along the creek at one point, and that ten miles above, there was another gathering spot of even greater interest.

---

3. Thomas Capanius Holm, *A Short Description of New Sweden*, 53.
4. Johann David Schoepf, *Travels in the Confederation*, 321.
5. Philip Tome, *Pioneer Life*, 55-58.

"Rattlesnake Pete" of Venango County.

Here, says Tome, was a large rock, "about forty feet long by fifteen feet wide, called Rattle-snake Rock, upon which the snakes would often lie in piles." At this same place, Tome notes that on the opposite bank of the creek (which he refers to as a river), there was another large rock "seventy feet long and twenty wide on which could often be seen forty snakes at a time!"[6]

He goes on to support this claim by recalling an experience two hunters had in 1794 when on a hunting expedition up Pine Creek. "About the third day," so says Tome in describing an event that must have occurred at Rattlesnake Rock, "they arrived at the larger rock on the west side of the river and found as many as thirty rattle-snakes lying on the rock sunning themselves. They pushed their canoe to the other shore, and when passing the smaller rock, they discovered on the top a pile of rattlesnakes as large

---

6. Ibid.

as an outdoor bake oven. They lay with their heads sticking up in every direction, hissing at them."[7]

To add further credence to his contention that rattlesnakes were amazingly abundant in his times, Tome recalls a first-hand experience he and his brother had while hunting and fishing along Pine Creek one afternoon in late August. Tome writes, "We were pushing up the river in our canoe and passed a rattlesnake's den, near which we counted forty rattlesnakes, some coiled up, and others stretched out, sunning themselves."[8]

What Tome says happened next will be discounted by some as more of Tome's tendency to embellish his accounts, but we'll look at this in some detail after recalling Tome's recollection.

"We went ashore and provided ourselves each with a stick made similar to a flail so that we could kill them with a single blow," he begins. "One then went below them, the other above, and we killed all we could until we met. We succeeded in killing thirty of the forty snakes which we first counted. In killing so many snakes, we inhaled so much of the poisonous effluvia as to make us sick. We returned home immediately and took freely of sweet milk and hog's lard to prevent any more serious effects."[9]

So, to shed some light on Tome's claims, we begin by looking at other historical accounts, which sometimes look somewhat exaggerated. In Miss Blackman's *History of Susquehanna County*, for example, events describe the prevalence of rattlesnakes noticed by pioneer settlers in that county around 1780, when, she says, "rattlesnakes sung in farmers' barns and made music" in their hay fields."[10]

Here, near present-day Red Rock, Luzerne County, one hot August afternoon, a group of huckleberry pickers, after filling their pails, "went to killing rattlesnakes." According to one first-hand account, the snake hunters killed, in the span of a few hours, a total of 444 rattlers, 411 of which were young ones.[11]

Another historian from northeastern Pennsylvania mentions that Elias Scott, one of the first settlers in the Lackawanna Valley in 1792, "found a

---
7. Ibid.
8. Ibid.
9. Ibid.
10. Emily Blackman, *History of Susquehanna County*, pp 106 & 57.
11. Ibid.

rattlesnake den on the upper waters of Spring Brook and killed 750 of the reptiles in a single day; the next day, he slew 375 more!"[12]

And yet another reliable historian recalls several events that reveal the multitude of rattlesnakes once found in northwestern Pennsylvania. The first episode he records concerns a Jefferson County farmer who found a rattlesnake den about a mile from his cabin. He and two other farmers attacked the reptiles, and supposedly, they "killed three hundred of them in two hours."[13]

That same historian also recounts another mind-blowing episode in Mercer County around 1803 or 1804. Early one morning, Mrs. John Johnson stepped outside her cabin to get her cows. She had not gone far until she heard the ominous rattles of snakes all around her.

Realizing she was probably in the middle of a large rattlesnake den, she knew she could not run through them. Seeing a large dogwood tree by her side, she climbed into its sturdy branches and cried for help.

Her strident cries soon brought her husband and a neighbor carrying stout hickory poles. The two men began wielding the clubs earnestly and soon cleared an escape route for Mrs. Johnson. They later piled up and counted the snakes they had killed and were surprised to realize that there "were two hundred in number."[14]

It would certainly not be a very pleasurable experience to stumble into a writhing mass of snakes, especially in difficult terrain or cramped quarters. However, such a thing can happen, as Sam Askey, the great pioneer panther hunter of Snow Shoe, Centre County, found out one day in the early nineteenth century.

On this particular occasion, Askey and Colonel John Holt, a fellow hunter, were returning from the "Big Moshannon licks" in the Allegheny Mountains. The men had killed some deer, and their horse was loaded with fresh venison. Just as they approached a ridge on the north side of Black Moshannon Creek near Snow Shoe, Askey's dog started barking excitedly. The little canine was somewhere off to the left and down at the bottom of

---

12. H. Hollister, *History of the Lackawanna Valley*, 284.
13. W. C. McKnight, *Pioneer Outline History*, 583.
14. Ibid.

A view of large and small Rattlesnake Rock, Tioga State Forest, Lycoming County, May 2023.

a hill where it couldn't be seen, so Askey decided to investigate, probably thinking there might be an opportunity for a shot at more wild game.

Askey left Holt behind to watch the horse and headed down the mountain. The intrepid hunter found a pile of large boulders on the way to the dog. Rather than skirt the extensive obstacle, he tried to make his way over it. He climbed up one particularly large rock and then decided to jump down a distance of about five feet to the ground below. When he did so, he landed in the middle of a rattlesnake den. In recalling the incident, Askey claimed that there were so many snakes all around him "that every step I made I tramped upon them. It seemed to me like tramping over beef entrails on a butchering day."[15]

But getting back to Philip Tome's claim that the "poisonous effluvia" from the rattlesnakes they had killed caused him and his brother to become ill. This claim seems implausible, but further research supports the account as historically accurate or in keeping with a popular belief of those times.

---

15. John Blair Linn, *History of Centre and Clinton Counties*, 422.

"It has always been said by old hunters and woodsmen," begins an interesting 1883 *New York Times* article, "that under certain conditions, a rattlesnake exudes an odor which is not only unbearably offensive to the sense of smell but that if a person should be subjected to its presence for any length of time in a close room, the result would be fatal to him. This has been generally looked upon as one of the many superstitions that prevail among the residents of the backwoods, but a case is reported from the Pocono region, which, if true, and it seems to be well-substantiated, would indicate that the belief is founded on fact."[16]

The article describes how two men from New Jersey were exploring some timberland in the Pocono Mountains near Stroudsburg, Monroe County, that they wanted to purchase. To add to the novelty of their adventure, they decided to spend one night in the open air by a campfire. But the night proved so cold that they decided to spend the night inside a deserted hunter's log cabin on the headwaters of Little Bushkill Creek.

Determined to enjoy that campfire they had looked forward to; they soon had a roaring fire in the cabin's fireplace. Stretching themselves out before the warm fire, they quickly fell asleep. Then, in the middle of the night, one was awakened with an oppressive weight on his chest and some difficulty breathing. He also noticed a "particularly sickening smell" that seemed to permeate the entire cabin.

With some difficulty, the drowsy man awakened his companion, who seemed to be breathing unsteadily. Both men were seized with dizziness and nausea upon attempting to stand, but they managed to get to the cabin door, which they struggled to open but finally succeeded. Upon staggering outside, they both fell to the ground and experienced violent fits of vomiting. After half an hour, they began to feel better, but they continued to feel weak and nervous until daylight.

Reluctant to reenter the cabin, they waited until broad daylight to do so, when upon entering, they could still smell the same peculiar odor that had driven them outside the night before. But now, in the morning light, they could also clearly see five large rattlesnakes stretched out on the hearth "not ten feet from where they had been sleeping."

---

16. "A Pennsylvania Snake Story," *The New York Times*, September 18, 1883, edition.

A rattler ready to strike. (ShutterStock photo)

The horrified men believed it was those same snakes that had emitted the odor that caused them to become sick, but being as afraid of the men as the men were of the snakes, the reptiles slithered away and quickly disappeared in chinks in the chimney and through cracks and holes in the floor.

The account says that the men did not try to kill the snakes, nor did they linger long, but instead "lost no time in reaching the nearest settlement." It is recalled that "they were enlightened as to the theory of the woodsmen's rattlesnake skin poison."[17]

Many superstitions like this may have had some basis in fact, including one such belief espoused by Philip Tome. He declared that snakes avoided any forest that had been burned over and that his family kept the area around their cabin cleared and burned off to keep them away.[18]

Similarly, herpetologists have shown that snakes emit an odor, particularly as a defense mechanism when threatened or even to attract a mate. The odor varies from snake to snake, but it is acknowledged that rattlesnakes

---

17. Ibid.
18. Philip Tome, *Pioneer Life*, 55-58.

A rattler sunning itself on the rocks (ShutterStock photo)

give off the most intense smell of all, with the odor being "musky and strong" and varying from that of rotting animal carcasses to cucumbers.[19]

Other historical accounts add further evidence to the contention that rattlesnakes were once so prevalent in Pennsylvania almost defied belief. Up in the mountainous wilds of Union Township near Howard in the northwestern corner of Centre County, for instance, the former Philadelphia and Erie Turnpike was referred to as the Rattlesnake Pike due to the prevalence of rattlesnakes that could once be found there, and present-day Route 504 still goes by that nickname today.[20]

But the human-interest side of this equation is also noteworthy. Rattlesnakes seem to have left some larger-than-life Pennsylvania snake hunters in their wake, with "Rattlesnake Pete" of Venango County and "Saint Patrick" of Perry County being remembered as the most notable.

Pete Gruber was the proverbial snake oil salesman. Often referred to as "one of the last old-time hunters and peddlers of rattlesnake oil," he was

---
19. "Snake, Rattle, and Roll: Pennsylvania Timber Rattlesnakes - Can you Smell a Snake – What do Snakes Smell, Stink Like," *Pennsylvania Heritage*, Winter 2019.
20. John Blair Linn, *History of Centre and Clinton Counties*, 446.

born in Oil City, Venango County, in 1858. His reputation as a rattlesnake hunter and snake oil salesman continued to grow as time went by, and eventually, this notoriety led locals to affectionately assign him the nickname "Rattlesnake Pete."

It was a nickname he relished and used to his advantage in his marketing endeavors. Often seen attired, from head to toe, in rattlesnake-skin clothes, he cut quite a picture as he was seen heading off on his rattlesnake hunts in his bright red convertible with its large brass snake-head hood ornament and his two large dogs peering out over the car doors.

Locals also were impressed with Pete's collection of rattlesnake rattles and skins, which he had acquired over the years. He also sold bottles of their venom and the fatty snake oil he extracted from them. It was a process he claimed he learned from an elderly Seneca Indian woman who lived on the Cornplanter Reservation.

He recalled that he met her on the trail hiking in the dense virgin forest near his home. She immediately drew his attention because she was dragging a large rattlesnake behind her—one of the largest he had ever seen. He engaged her in a friendly conversation and inquired about what she intended to do with the large reptile.

The old lady was quite taken with the young man's interest and readily explained how she could extract the snake's fatty oil and how effective it was for treating many common ailments, including rheumatism, arthritis, and others. Impressed by his questions, the elderly Indian even gave the young man the snake's skin. He later said that through this lady's friendship, he befriended Seneca medicine men who taught him how to utilize the snake's rattles to cure other human ailments.

Pete was also hailed as the man to go to if a rattler bit you. He had developed a method of making an anti-venom, which he used to save the life of a circus clown and treat the 29 rattlesnake bites he incurred during his many years of hunting the venomous serpents. In the end, old age claimed him, not rattlesnakes. He was 74 years old when he passed in 1932.[21]

Perry County had its version of Rattlesnake Pete, and he was also skilled at capturing rattlers, even though he feared them. Irvin George achieved

---

21. Joe Nickell, The Story of "Rattlesnake Pete," from Centerforinquiry.org/blog website, based on Arch Merrill's book titled *Shadows on the Wall*, published 1952.

Rattlesnake Rocks - a view from the other side looking up Pine Creek.

some degree of fame for his rattlesnake handling and captures. He was almost as flamboyant about it as Rattlesnake Pete of Venango County.

In the late 19th and early 20th century, George claimed it was his duty to kill or capture every rattlesnake or copperhead he could find because it meant it might eventually save someone from being bitten by those venomous vipers. He also liked to display those kills, with his neighbors often remarking about seeing him driving by in his horse and cart with captured snakes tied to the wheels.

Although those neighbors may have chuckled about his unusual habits behind his back, they must have admired George's pluck, evident from the many snakebite scars that covered his arms. They also must have felt grateful for his one-man war against poisonous snakes. They showed gratitude in the nickname they gave him. Recalling the Irish legend claiming it was Saint Patrick who rid the Emerald Isle of snakes, the Perry County folks decided Irvin George should have the identical honorary title of "Saint Patrick of Perry County."

The Irish legend states that when first landing on the island to begin missionary work, Saint Patrick was appalled by the number of snakes there. After being attacked by a group of them and recalling that serpents are pictured as a symbol of the devil in the Bible, he decided he needed to cleanse the island nation of all serpents. He "shooed every legless reptile he could find into the ocean."[22]

Scholars who have examined the Saint Patrick legend have decided it's just that: a legendary account with no basis in fact. They knew that the Emerald Isle was covered with thick sheets of ice during the Ice Age, precluding any wildlife, including snakes.

After the glaciers melted and the island became inhabitable again, animals from surrounding islands and the mainland swam to it and reestablished themselves there. However, snakes cannot swim, and even if they could have done so, they would not have survived the cold waters of the Atlantic Ocean. So, the scholars who examined the Saint Patrick legend concluded that "Saint Patrick had nothing to do with Ireland's snakelessness."[23]

Therefore, it seems that Irvin George has a greater claim to ridding Potter County of snakes than Saint Patrick does of eliminating them from Ireland. It is not a trivial accomplishment for a little-known snake hunter from the mountains of northern Pennsylvania.

LOCATION: **Rattlesnake Rock** is beside Pine Creek near the village of Cedar Run along Route 414. Across the creek towers Cedar Mountain, part of Tioga State Forest on the border of Tioga and Lycoming Counties. (DD GPS Coordinates: 41.520164586 -77.44083157). From Lock Haven, follow 220 North to Jersey Shore. Pick up 44 North and follow to a right-hand turnoff onto Route 414 shortly after passing through Waterville. Follow Route 414 through Slate Run and then through Cedar Run. Continue for about two miles, looking for the Rattlesnake Rock Access pull-off on the right. There is a well-marked, easy downhill trail through pine woods to get to Pine Creek and Rattlesnake Rock.

---

22. Jason Bittel, "Did Saint Patrick get rid of the snakes in Ireland?" Article in *The Washington Post*, March 14, 2021.
23. Ibid.

UNBELIEVABLE POSTSCRIPT

During a book signing at Restless Oaks Restaurant near McElhatten, Clinton County, in June of 2023, I was talking to one of the owners of the popular eating establishment. My affable friend Jim Maguire Junior shared a remarkable story after I told him about my recent trip to Rattlesnake Rock and how I learned about it through reading Philip Tome's interesting history titled *Pioneer Life, or Thirty Years a Hunter*.

When I mentioned Philip Tome and Tome's mention of Rattlesnake Rock, my friend said that he bought the property on which the Tome family homestead was once located and had built a hunting cabin upon it. But his account of what happened when building the cabin proved to be the most remarkable part of his tale.

He recalled that when clearing land for his cabin, they had to cut down a lot of trees, and when cutting down one gigantic hollow tree, they encountered something that would most likely send shudders up the spines of the most seasoned woodsmen.

Mr. Maguire noted that as the tree began to fall, a sudden outburst of black snakes, almost too numerous to count, poured out from its hollow cavity. But following that emergence, there then came the head of another that seemed to be of impossible size. The huge snake slowly slithered out and then over to a nearby tree and ascended it. The men building the cabin were dumbfounded, but one finally snapped a photo of the snake (See the picture provided by Mr. Maguire).

Then, after getting closer, they got a good idea of its length, which they set at eleven feet! To this day, they still can hardly believe what they saw, especially when they also estimated the circumference of the snake's body to be almost twenty inches! Philip Tome would have been impressed, and he may have even claimed he once saw a rattlesnake that was just as long!

The elven foot long blacksnake that would no doubt have even amazed veteran hunter Phillip Tome!

BIBLIOGRAPHY

Aldrich, Lewis Cass, *History of Clearfield County, Pennsylvania*, D. Mason & Co., Syracuse, N. Y., 1887.

Ashe, Thomas, *Travels in America*, performed in 1806, Richard Phillips Publishing, London, 1808, Republished by Badgley Publishing Co., Canal Winchester, Ohio, 2012. (All page number references to Ashe's book in the footnotes are the page numbers found in Badgley's republished volume.)

Bristow, Arch, *Old Time Tales of Warren County*, Warren County Historical Society, Warren, Pa. 1932.

Cummings, Uriah, *Song of U-RI-ON-TAH*, Courier Co., Buffalo, N. Y., 1900.

Dorson, Richard M., *American Folklore and the Historian*, The University of Chicago Press, Chicago, Ill., 1971.

Grimm, Jacob, *Teutonic Mythology*, George Bell & Sons, London, 1882.

Heindel, Ned D., *Hexenkopf History, Healing & Hexerei*, Northampton County Genealogical and Historical Society, Easton, Pa., 2009.

Hollister, H., *History of the Lackawanna Valley*, M. Norton, bookseller and stationer, Scranton, Pa., 1875.

Holm, Thomas Campanius, *Description of the province of New Sweden. Now called by the English, Pennsylvania in America*, translated from the Swedish by Peter S. du Ponceau, McCarty & Davis, Philadelphia, 1834.

Linn, John Blair, *History of Centre and Clinton Counties, Pennsylvania*, Louis H. Everts Co., 1883.

Maynard, D. S., *Historical View of Clinton County*, Enterprise Printing House, Lock Haven, Pa. 1875.

McKnight, William J., *Pioneer Outline History of Northwestern Pennsylvania*, Lippincott Co., Philadelphia., 1905.

Michaux, Francois, *Travels to the West of the Allegheny Mountains*, London, 1805. Reprint edition by Applewood Books, Carlisle, Mass., 2012.

Rung, Albert M., *Rung's Chronicles of PA History*, Huntingdon County Historical Society, Huntingdon, Pa.

Schoepf, Johann David, *Travels in the Confederation, 1783-1784*, Afred J. Morrison, Philadelphia, 1911.
Stevenson, Whitcomb Fletcher, *Pennsylvania Agriculture And Country Life, 1640-1840*, Pennsylvania Museum and Historical Commission, Harrisburg, 1971.
Swanger, Rebecca, "The Root of the Forestry Movement in Pennsylvania: J. T. Rothrock," *Pennsylvania Magazine of History and Biography, Vol. CXXXIV*, No. 4 (October 2010).
Tome, Philip, *Pioneer Life, or Thirty Years a Hunter*, published for the author, Buffalo, N.Y., 1834.
Trento, Salvatore, *The Search for Lost America: The Mysteries of the Stone Ruins*, Contemporary Books, Chicago, 1978.
Wall, Thomas. L., *Clearfield County Pennsylvania Present and Past*. Self-published, Clearfield, Pa., 1925.
Wallace, Paul A., *Indians Paths of Pennsylvania*, Pennsylvania Historical Commission, Harrisburg, 1971.
Welfley, William H. and Blackburn, E. Howard, *History of Bedford and Somerset Counties, Pennsylvania*, Hon. William H. Koontz, editor, Lewis Publishing Co., New York and Chicago, 1906.
Wrobel, Murray, editor, *Elsevier's Dictionary of Mammals*, Elsevier Science, London, 2006.

ABOUT THE AUTHOR

JEFFREY R. FRAZIER is author of eight books in a series titled *Pennsylvania Fireside Tales*. To many folks the title evokes images of an old log cabin sitting somewhere in an isolated and little-settled valley sowmewhere in the Pennsylvania mountains seventy-five or more years ago. A crackling fire in an ancient stone fireplace makes the interior a cozy place to be on a cold winter's night, especially in those unhurried days before electricity and automobiles forever changed the times that we now refer to as the "Good Old Days".

No television, radios or computers to break the monotony of the long evenings in those days. Entertainment then was often provided by an old patriarch sitting in his special chair in front of the fireplace. Surrounded by youngsters anxious to hear tales of the olden days, he would begin to talk about Indians, hunters who trailed the wolf and the mountain lion, ghosts, witches, gypsies, moonshiners, and other characters of the long ago; tales the author describes as the "soul" of these dark and rugged hills that we call home. It is these stories that Mister Frazier preserves in his books.

The author was born and raised in Centre Hall, Centre County, where he says he grew up in a "Tom Sawyer sort of way". Some of his fondest memories of that boyhood include explorations of out-of-the-way spots in the mountains and accounts of the legends that seem to cling to them. After graduating from Penn State in 1967 and moving out of state, he realized how much he loved the Pennsylvania mountains and their stories. It was this "home-sickness" that inspired him to collect and write the old-time tales. Since that time he has collected those same anecdotes from all over the state, ranging from the Blue Mountains of Berks and Lehigh Counties, the South Mountains of Adams County, the "Black Forest" area of Potter and Tioga Counties, the Alleghenies of Clearfield and Blair Counties, and the other counties in the middle.

Many of the stories often sound "far-fetched" to us today, but Mr. Frazier also tries to find the kernels of truth that might be buried in them. In that way he takes on the role of an investigative reporter or detective, treating each tale as a little mystery. It is because of this approach that he chose "Origins and Foundations of Pennsylvania Mountain Folktales, Legends, and Folklore" as the subtitle for his series of books. Written in a format that the average reader can enjoy, the tales take the reader back to a crackling fire in that cabin nestled among the green valleys of Pennsylvania's legend-shrouded mountains.

He also, at the urging of his readers, published a book titled *Pennsylvania Fireside Ghost Tales*. The stories therein should prove particularly appealing to lovers of both the natural and supernatural attractions Pennsylvania has to offer. In addition to his new three volume series titled *Pennsylvania Mountain Landmarks*, published by Sunbury Press, updated and expanded versions of all eight of his *Pennsylvania Fireside Tales* volumes and his *Pennsylvania Fireside Ghost Tales* will also be published by that same publisher.

Mr. Frazier also is available for speaking engagements. His lectures, titled "Pennsylvania Legends and Folktales – Fact or Fancy," include a PowerPoint presentation that enhances the old-time legends and folktales he talks about and which are chosen specifically for the area where he is invited to speak.

www.ingramcontent.com/pod-product-compliance
Lightning Source LLC
LaVergne TN
LVHW011423080426
835512LV00005B/236